Napoleon's Imperial Guard

Napoleon's Imperial Guard

Organization, Uniforms and Weapons

Gabriele Esposito

Pen & Sword
MILITARY

First published in Great Britain in 2021
by Pen & Sword Military
An imprint of Pen & Sword Books Limited
47 Church Street
Barnsley
South Yorkshire
S70 2AS

Copyright © Gabriele Esposito 2021

ISBN 978 1 52678 671 5

The right of Gabriele Esposito to be identified as
Author of this Work has been asserted by him in accordance
with the Copyright, Designs and Patents Act 1988.

A CIP catalogue record for this book is
available from the British Library

All rights reserved. No part of this book may be reproduced or
transmitted in any form or by any means, electronic or mechanical
including photocopying, recording or by any information storage and
retrieval system, without permission from the Publisher in writing.

Typeset in Adobe Caslon
by Mac Style

Printed and bound in India by Replika Press Pvt. Ltd.

Pen & Sword Books Limited incorporates the imprints of Atlas,
Archaeology, Aviation, Discovery, Family History, Fiction, History, Maritime,
Military, Military Classics, Politics, Select, Transport,
True Crime, Air World, Frontline Publishing, Leo Cooper,
Remember When, Seaforth Publishing, The Praetorian Press, Wharncliffe Local
History, Wharncliffe Transport,
Wharncliffe True Crime and White Owl.

For a complete list of Pen & Sword titles please contact
PEN & SWORD BOOKS LIMITED
47 Church Street, Barnsley, South Yorkshire, S70 2AS, England
E-mail: enquiries@pen-and-sword.co.uk
Website: www.pen-and-sword.co.uk

Contents

Acknowledgements ix
Introduction xi

Chapter 1   The Consular Guard   1
Chapter 2   The Foot Grenadiers and Foot Chasseurs   16
Chapter 3   The Infantry of the Middle Guard and Young Guard   37
Chapter 4   The Mounted Grenadiers   56
Chapter 5   The Mounted Chasseurs   65
Chapter 6   The Empress' Dragoons   77
Chapter 7   The Polish Lancers   86
Chapter 8   The Dutch Lancers   95
Chapter 9   The German Lancers and the Lithuanian Lancers   99
Chapter 10   The Guards of Honour and the Scouts   104
Chapter 11   The Mamelukes and the Tatars   117
Chapter 12   The Sailors and the Gendarmerie   125
Chapter 13   The Artillery and the Train   134

Bibliography 145
Index 147

Gabriele Esposito is a military historian who works as a freelance author and researcher for some of the most important publishing houses in the military history sector. In particular, he is an expert specializing in uniformology: his interests and expertise range from the ancient civilizations to modern post-colonial conflicts. During recent years he has conducted and published several researches on the military history of the Latin American countries, with special attention on the War of the Triple Alliance and the War of the Pacific. He is among the leading experts on the military history of the Italian Wars of Unification and the Spanish Carlist Wars. His books and essays are published on a regular basis by Osprey Publishing, Winged Hussar Publishing and Libreria Editrice Goriziana; he is also the author of numerous military history articles appearing in specialized magazines like *Ancient Warfare Magazine, Medieval Warfare Magazine, Classic Arms & Militaria Magazine, History of War, Guerres et Histoire, Focus Storia* and *Focus Storia Wars*.

Acknowledgements

This book is dedicated to my parents, Maria Rosaria and Benedetto, for all the great help that they give me during the creation of my books. A very special thanks goes to Philip Sidnell, my commissioning editor at Pen & Sword, for his precious support and advice. The quality of my books is the result of great teamwork, during which the production manager Matt Jones and the excellent Tony Walton play a crucial role. All the pictures published in this book are public domain ones obtained from the magnificent Digital Collections of the New York Public Library, in particular from the incredible Vinkhuijzen Collection of Military Uniforms. The vast contents of the latter can easily be browsed at: https://digitalcollections.nypl.org/collections/the-vinkhuijzen-collection-of-military-uniforms#/?tab=navigation.

Introduction

The main aim of this book is to present a detailed overview of the history, organization and uniforms of Napoleon's Imperial Guard. This elite corps was created in 1799 with the official denomination of Consular Guard, soon after Bonaparte became the First Consul of France. In 1804, with the proclamation of the French Empire, it assumed the new denomination with which it became famous, the Imperial Guard. During most of its history, the Imperial Guard of the French Army comprised three main echelons: the Old Guard, the Middle Guard and the Young Guard. The Old Guard was formed from veteran units that already existed before 1805 and whose soldiers had followed Napoleon since his first military campaigns of 1796/97. The Middle Guard was made up of younger veterans, who fought under Napoleon during the first victorious campaigns of the Empire (1805–09). The Young Guard comprised units that were organized after 1809 and whose members were young recruits; these were chosen from the annual intake of conscripts and volunteers who were recruited in the French Army. As we will see, these three main echelons included several units made up of foreign soldiers who served under Napoleon because of their sense of loyalty towards the emperor. In 1804, at its formation, the Imperial Guard comprised only some 8,000 soldiers; by 1812, at the beginning of the Russian campaign, it had ballooned to almost 100,000 soldiers and was an army corps comprising units from all the branches of service of the French Army. In many respects it was a true 'Praetorian' corps, having many privileges, but it should be remembered that Bonaparte's guardsmen always fought with great professionalism and courage when required to do so. The chapters of this book cover all the units that made up the Imperial Guard, from the most familiar contingents to the lesser-known corps.

Chapter 1

The Consular Guard

The French Army had always comprised a very large Royal Guard, which was commonly known as the Maison du Roi, or Household of the King. This consisted of several different units, both on foot and mounted, which were charged with the protection of the French royal family. The Royal Guard had been greatly expanded at the end of the seventeenth century, during Louis XIV's long reign. The famous Sun King transformed his own Royal Guard into a sort of miniature army that was made up of several military corps. These could be merely 'ceremonial' – i.e. small units wearing picturesque old-fashioned uniforms and being of little practical use – or larger combat corps that could be employed as elite troops during the military campaigns fought by the French Army. The French Royal Guard comprised the following units at the beginning of the eighteenth century:

- **Gardes de la Porte:** a single company of fifty foot guardsmen, guarding the inside of the Royal Palace
- **Cent-Gardes Suisses:** a single company of 100 Swiss foot guardsmen, guarding the Royal Rooms
- **Gardes de la Prevote:** a single company of eighty foot guardsmen, charged with police duties inside the Royal Palace
- **Gardes de la Manche:** twenty-five chosen guardsmen, who formed the inner bodyguard of the monarch
- **Gardes du Corps:** four companies of mounted bodyguards, the first of which was made up of Scottish soldiers. Each company had 400 men
- **Compagnie des Gendarmes:** one company of 200 heavy cavalrymen
- **Compagnie des Chevaux-Légers:** one company of 200 light cavalrymen
- **Mousquetaires du Roi:** two companies of musketeers with 150 men each, known as 'Grey' and 'Black' from the colours of their horses
- **Grenadiers à Cheval:** one company with 250 horse grenadiers, chosen from the best grenadiers of the French Army
- **Gardes Françaises:** an elite infantry regiment with thirty companies of 200 men each, assembled into six battalions plus two independent companies of grenadiers

- **Gardes Suisses:** an elite infantry regiment made up of Swiss mercenaries, with twelve companies of 200 men each (assembled into two battalions)
- **Gendarmerie de France:** sixteen companies of 'territorial' heavy cavalry, recruited from the aristocrats living in the various provinces of France. Each company could have from a minimum of eighty to a maximum of 200 horsemen, and acted as a reserve for the other cavalry units of the Royal Guard

During the period 1775–88, in order to significantly cut the costs of the Royal Household, several of the smaller corps were disbanded: the Mousquetaires du Roi in 1775; the Grenadiers à Cheval in 1776; the Gardes de la Porte, the Compagnie des Gendarmes and the Compagnie des Chevaux-Légers in 1787; and the Gendarmerie de France in 1788. When the French Revolution broke out in 1789, the six remaining units of the Royal Guard had different destinies. The Cent-Gardes Suisses remained on active service until 1790, but were disbanded two years later, while the Gardes de la Manche and the Gardes du Corps were both disbanded in 1791 after the historical episode known as the 'March on Versailles', during which an angry crowd of poor Parisian citizens marched on the Royal Palace of Versailles, with the intention of killing the royal family and seizing food from the stores of the royal court. The attack on Versailles was also partly caused by the behaviour of the Gardes du Corps, which had organized a rich banquet during the previous days in order to welcome the members of another military unit that had been transferred to Paris.

The Gardes Françaises and the Gardes Suisses were the two largest combat units of the Royal Guard and, as such, they had all the necessary military potential to influence the political events that took place in Paris during the early months of the French Revolution. Soon after the outbreak of the first uprising, the French Guards joined the cause of the rebels and supported them during the famous assault on the Bastille; without having the professional soldiers of the Gardes Françaises among their ranks, the civilian insurgents in Paris would have never been able to conquer the infamous fortress-prison. After these bloody events, since the king no longer had trust in them, the Gardes Françaises were disbanded on 31 August 1789. Most of the members of this elite unit had strong personal links with the local community in Paris, and consequently joined the embryonic National Guard that had been created just a few weeks before. The National Guard was a completely new military organization, recruited from all those French citizens who wished to defend the ideals of the Revolution. Thanks to the incorporation of many former professional soldiers from the French Guards, the National Guard soon became an effective fighting force that kept order on the streets of Paris. The soldiers of the Swiss Guards were all professionals, mercenaries who had signed a contract with the French monarch and who were extremely loyal to Louis. When the Gardes Françaises deserted and joined the insurgents, the Swiss soldiers continued to serve the royal family with their usual professionalism and pride. Being foreigners and having signed a contract with the French state, they could not be easily disbanded by the new revolutionary government like the other units of the Royal Household. The Swiss Guards started to be perceived by the population of Paris as a potential menace to the stability of their new constitutional government; as a result, the Gardes Suisses became particularly hated across the French capital. On 10 August 1792, a crowd of citizens marched on and stormed the Royal Palace of the Tuileries, which was located in the centre of Paris. The imposing building was garrisoned at the time by the Swiss Guards, who retreated to the gardens at the rear of it to face the insurgents. The professional soldiers fought with enormous courage against the crowd, until the king ordered them to put down their weapons; several Swiss guardsmen, who were captured during the fight, were later executed. After these bloody events, the Gardes Suisses also ceased to exist. In September 1791, while France was still a monarchy but had already promulgated a constitution, an attempt was made to create a new Constitutional Guard of the King. This body comprised most of the soldiers from the disbanded corps of the Royal Household and protected both the monarch and the new constitution. The Constitutional Guard of the King had a total of 1,300 infantrymen and 600 cavalry, organized in three infantry divisions with eight fifty-man companies each and three cavalry divisions with four fifty-man companies each. In May 1792, after only a short existence, the Constitutional Guard was disbanded.

By September 1792 only the Gardes de la Prevote were still active; on 10 May 1791, however, this body had changed its name and received new tasks. Before the outbreak of the Revolution, this company of foot guardsmen had acted as a sort of military police inside the buildings of the French royal family; after the creation of the National Assembly, the first parliament in the history of France, its ninety members were ordered to act as the new Guard of the Legislative Corps. In practice, they had to defend the members of the parliament and guard the room where the National Assembly took its decisions. It soon became clear that a single company was not enough to protect the new parliament, and thus the Guard of the Legislative Corps was expanded to two companies. After the destruction of the Swiss Guards in August 1792, the former Gardes de la Prevote were reorganized and received the new denomination of Grenadier Corps of the National Gendarmerie. Although the uniform of the corps was changed, its internal structure remained the same. In June 1793, the National Assembly – by now known as the National Convention – was attacked by a group of extremist insurgents. During these events, the Grenadiers-Gendarmes refused to act and several of them joined the attackers; consequently, they earned a very bad reputation and were subsequently deprived of most of their functions. On 29 June 1795, the revolutionary government of France decided to reorganize its guard corps, which now once again received the old denomination of Guard of the Legislative Corps. According to the new reorganization, the corps was to have a large establishment with 800 men in eight grenadier companies. At this time the Legislative Corps was strongly menaced by several groups of political extremists and thus a guard unit that could protect it was absolutely vital. As a result, in October 1795, the Guard of the Legislative Corps was expanded from eight to twelve companies of grenadiers, having a total of 1,250 privates.

The government of revolutionary France assumed a new organization in November 1795 and started to be known as the Directorate, a five-member committee which gained power after the fall of Robespierre. After three years of massacres and revolts, the Directorate tried to restore order in France and to limit the power of the various political factions that had emerged from the events of 1792–95. The members of this committee quickly started to rule the country as a virtual oligarchy, and in consequence the number of their enemies rapidly increased. As a result of this, a new Guard of the Executive Directorate was created in October 1796 for the protection of the Directorate. This military corps comprised 240 men, organized into four companies: two of foot grenadiers and two of horse grenadiers. In comparison with the Guard of the Legislative Corps, the Guard of the Directorate was much smaller, but unlike the former it also comprised some cavalrymen who could act as a mounted bodyguard.

On 9 November 1799, after returning from his Egyptian campaign, Napoleon took power in France with a military coup and installed a new form of government known as the Consulate. France, which had been a republic for several years, was now to be governed by a triumvirate that was under the orders of the ambitious and victorious Corsican general. Indeed, Napoleon was soon proclaimed perpetual First Consul, and could therefore exert his dominance over the other two members of the triumvirate. Just two days after becoming the new master of France, on 11 November 1799, Napoleon decided to create a new military corps known as the Consular Guard, which was to protect the three consuls and the new form of government from internal menaces such as revolts or coups. This force was to be formed by men who were extremely loyal to Napoleon and had already fought under him in Italy or Egypt. The Consular Guard, however, was not created out of nothing, but rather by assembling together the two guard corps that already existed in France: the Guard of the Directorate and the Guard of the Legislative Corps. The new corps was much stronger than the two previous units because it absorbed a large number of skilled veterans. According to its initial structure, the Consular Guard created by Napoleon comprised the following units:

Soldiers of the Mounted Grenadiers (Consular Guard) in campaign dress with *surtout*.

- Two battalions of foot grenadiers
- One company of foot chasseurs (light infantry)
- Two squadrons of mounted grenadiers
- One company of mounted chasseurs (light cavalry)
- One company of light artillery (with horse-drawn guns)

From the outset, the Consular Guard was characterized by the presence of sub-units from all branches of service of the French Army: it was Napoleon's intention

Soldier of the Mounted Chasseurs (Consular Guard) with second uniform.

to create a miniature army comprising every kind of military unit (infantry, cavalry and artillery). As we have seen, this was not a new concept, since the Maison du Roi of the French monarchs had always comprised both foot and mounted corps; it was only with Napoleon, however, that the French Army started to include some artillery units with 'guard' status. The First Consul of France had initiated his brilliant military career as an artillery officer, so always paid special attention to the artillery corps of his army. During Napoleon's second Italian campaign, in 1800, the Consular Guard fought with enormous valour against the Austrians at the decisive Battle of Marengo, demonstrating that it was one of the best combat units in the French Army. Differently from the other guard corps created in post-1789 France, it was trained and equipped to fight as an elite force and not merely to perform static garrison duties. In September 1800, after the victory at Marengo, the First Consul decided to expand his Guard: the foot chasseurs became a battalion, a third squadron was added to the mounted grenadiers and a second company was added to the mounted chasseurs. As a result of this expansion, the Consular Guard now comprised some 3,600 soldiers. Napoleon, however, was still not satisfied with its strength, and continued to enlarge his guard units during the following years.

During 1801–02, the Consular Guard was expanded with the addition of two new corps. The first was a company made up of 140 veteran soldiers, who were no longer fit for active service but could perform garrison duties; the second consisted of a legion of Gendarmes, a militarized police that was tasked with keeping order in the French Army as well as in the various provinces of France. The Mounted Chasseurs were expanded to two squadrons in 1801 and were thereby reorganized as a proper light cavalry regiment. Since the foundation of the Consular Guard, the Mounted Chasseurs had formed the horse bodyguard of Napoleon, who held them in great esteem and usually wore their dark green service dress as his own personal uniform. The Mounted Grenadiers, who already had an establishment with two squadrons, were also reorganized as a proper regiment. The Foot Chasseurs, meanwhile were expanded to two battalions in order to have the same numerical consistency as the Foot Grenadiers. Both units were restructured as regiments and received new official denominations: Corps of the Foot Grenadiers and Corps of the Foot Chasseurs. By the end of 1802, after the great expansion described above, the Consular Guard had a total of 5,300 soldiers. By that time, in order to be admitted into the ranks of the Guard, a French soldier had to be a veteran of at least three military campaigns and be a decorated fighter. As a result, only the best and most loyal soldiers could make up the units of the Consular Guard. The Foot Grenadiers were the elite of the Guard, since their members had to be at least 1.8 metres tall and were chosen according to their personal loyalty towards Napoleon. The First Consul added another three units to his Guard before becoming emperor of the French in 1804: the Mamelukes, the Sailors and the Velites.

At the time of Napoleon's Egyptian campaign in 1798, Egypt was still part of the Ottoman Empire but was ruled by a local military caste whose members were known as Mamelukes. The Mamelukes had originally been an independent dynasty that had ruled Egypt during the Middle Ages, until they were defeated and conquered by the Ottoman Turks at the beginning of the sixteenth century. Initially, the Mamelukes were non-Muslim slaves who were employed as professional soldiers by the various Islamic states of the Middle Ages; they later converted to Islam and became a caste of free warriors. After conquering Egypt, they defended their new homeland from the Mongol invasions and even expelled the last Crusaders from the Holy Land. After being conquered by the Ottomans, the Mamelukes were able to retain a high degree of autonomy and thus continued to rule Egypt, albeit – at least formally – as vassals of the Turks. The arrival of the French Army, under the command of Napoleon, caused great political changes in Egypt. The military power of the Mamelukes was destroyed by the French at the Battle of the Pyramids (1798), and the Ottomans had to rely on English military help in order to reconquer Egypt in 1800. After the military events of 1799–1800, the Mamelukes practically ceased to exist as a military caste. Napoleon, however, had been impressed by their enormous courage during the Battle of the Pyramids, and thus decided to accept some of them inside his military forces. The Mamelukes fought as excellent light cavalrymen, armed with flintlock pistols and deadly sabres; during the Battle of the Pyramids they attacked the French infantry with an impressive frontal charge but were massacred by the deadly fire delivered by Napoleon's troops, which were deployed in defensive squares. When Napoleon left Egypt, a certain number of Mamelukes decided to follow him back to France. Here they were organized into a light cavalry company of 124 men, who served together with the Mounted Chasseurs of the Consular Guard as the horse bodyguard of the First Consul. The Mamelukes took their families with them to France and soon became famous for their loyalty towards Napoleon, which could appear fanatical to contemporary observers. The company of Mamelukes, organized on 13 October 1801, was later expanded to become a squadron with two companies thanks to the arrival of new recruits from the Levant. Like all the members of the Consular Guard, the Mamelukes received higher pay than the ordinary soldiers of the French Army and lived in comfortable barracks. One of them, the famous Roustam Raza, was the personal servant of Napoleon, who had a very special relationship with Raza and considered him more as a friend than a bodyguard.

The Sailors of the Consular Guard were created in 1803, soon after hostilities between France and Great Britain resumed, the conflict having been temporarily

Mameluke of the Consular Guard.

suspended by the Peace of Amiens, which had been signed just a few months before. In 1803, Napoleon, deciding that the right moment had come to attempt an invasion of Britain, deployed his forces in northern France, in order to prepare them for the crossing of the English Channel. The First Consul was sure that the British Army would prove no match for his veteran soldiers, but had one great problem: the Royal Navy controlled all the seas of the world and was much stronger than the French Navy. Without adequate support from his naval forces, Napoleon would have never been able to cross the Channel with his army. Consequently, the French Navy was ordered to distract the British fleet for as long as possible to enable the invading force to cross the sea without significant opposition. However, the French Navy could not carry out Napoleon's orders and his land forces remained on the continent: the invasion never did materialize, the final nail in its coffin being Nelson's crushing victory over a combined Franco-Spanish fleet off Cape Trafalgar in October 1805. During his military preparations, however, Napoleon created a special corps of sailors that was made part of the Consular Guard and was retained in service after the invasion of Britain was cancelled. This unit, a battalion of naval infantry, was originally formed to act as the naval bodyguard of the First Consul; it would have served on the warship that would transport Napoleon during the crossing of the English Channel. The Battalion of Sailors consisted of 730 men, recruited from the best elements of the French Navy. It was organized on five sub-units, known as *equipages*, each of which could act in an autonomous way and could be embarked on a different warship. The 'matelots', or sailors, of this corps were trained as naval infantrymen and were equipped as assault troops; in case of need, they could board enemy ships. In time of peace, they were charged with escorting the First Consul when he moved by river or sea.

The Velites of the Consular Guard were the last unit to be organized before the Consular Guard was transformed into the Imperial Guard, being created on 24 September 1804. During Antiquity, the Latin term '*velites*' was employed to identify the light infantrymen of the Republican Roman Army; over time, it started to be used to indicate the young cadets who were at the beginning of their military career. The Velites of the Consular Guard were organized on two battalions, with five companies each. Differently from the Foot Grenadiers and Foot Chasseurs, however, they did not form an independent regiment. Their first battalion was attached to the Corps of Foot Grenadiers and their second battalion to the Corps of Foot Chasseurs. The members of this new corps were all young soldiers, with little military experience but with a solid personal reputation; they had to come from rich families and have had a sound education. From the beginning, the two battalions of the Velites were intended to act as a sort of training corps: their young members would have learned a lot from serving side-by-side with the veterans of the Consular Guard's other infantry units. After becoming experienced soldiers, the Velites were to be transferred to the Foot Grenadiers and Foot Chasseurs, or enter the line regiments as junior officers. This basic idea would be further developed by Napoleon during the following years, when the Consular Guard was transformed into the Imperial Guard. Young soldiers learned from experience and served alongside veterans from the beginning of their military career. This concept would later result in the organization of the Imperial Guard into three main branches: the Old Guard, Middle Guard and Young Guard.

Shortly before Napoleon's coronation as Emperor of the French, the Consular Guard comprised the following units:

Quartermaster of the Sailors (Consular Guard) in campaign dress.

- The Corps of Foot Grenadiers, on two battalions
- The Corps of Foot Chasseurs, on two battalions
- The Corps of the Velites, on two battalions
- The Regiment of Mounted Grenadiers, on two squadrons
- The Regiment of Mounted Chasseurs, on two squadrons
- The Squadron of Mamelukes
- The Company of Light Artillery
- The Battalion of Sailors
- The Legion of Gendarmes

During 1804, the single Company of Light Artillery was expanded and transformed into a squadron with two companies, always equipped with light horse-drawn guns. The Legion of Gendarmes, also known as the Elite Gendarmerie of the Consular Guard, consisted of three sub-units: two mounted squadrons with two companies each and one foot half-battalion with two companies. The 630 members of the Gendarmerie performed a series of important tasks: they were the military police of the Consular Guard and had to protect all the locations where the First Consul and his personal staff moved during military operations. Although in case of war the Elite Gendarmerie could not be employed as normal combat troops, on several occasions, they fought with great courage, despite not being required to do so. All members of this corps were chosen from the best elements of France's National Gendarmerie, the large military police force that kept order in the French provinces.

Before concluding this first chapter dedicated to the Consular Guard, it is necessary to present a short overview of another military unit that acted as Napoleon's personal escort during his early military career: the Guides of Bonaparte. During the Revolutionary Wars of 1792–1800, most of the French generals had small corps of guides at their direct orders. These usually consisted of a few light cavalrymen, who were employed to transmit orders to subordinate commanders or to explore the enemy territory during marches. Sometimes these guides could also act as the mounted bodyguards of their general and his personal staff. The young Napoleon, like all the other French generals, had his own corps of guides. This was created in September 1796 and initially consisted of just 160 light cavalrymen, assembled into a single squadron. Napoleon was fighting in northern Italy against the Austrians at that time, and was gaining the first significant victories of his career. During this period, the Guides of Bonaparte accompanied him on every occasion and provided him with a reliable escort. By 1797, the original corps had been expanded to four squadrons and also included twenty-six gunners with two artillery pieces, along with two light infantry companies from another small corps of guides that were absorbed

Soldier of the Consular Guard's Mounted Artillery.

Officer of the Mounted Guides of Bonaparte.

into Napoleon's guides. As a result, like the future Consular Guard, the Guides comprised soldiers from all branches of service of the French Army. When Napoleon launched his Egyptian campaign, the Guides followed him to North Africa, where they distinguished themselves on several occasions, fighting in the desert with enormous courage. During the Egyptian campaign, the corps was restructured on ten companies – five of light cavalry and five of light infantry – supported by a detachment with sixty gunners. Two companies (one of cavalry and one of infantry) were defined as 'auxiliary', since they were formed by soldiers who had been recruited in Egypt from the local communities. Also attached to the Guides of Bonaparte were some Egyptian guides, semi-regular scouts who were not part of any company. When Napoleon abandoned Egypt, the survivors of the Guides of Bonaparte followed him to France, where these veterans were absorbed into the new Consular Guard, making up part of the Foot Chasseurs and Horse Chasseurs.

Chapter 2

The Foot Grenadiers and Foot Chasseurs

History and organization

On 14 May 1804, Napoleon crowned himself Emperor of the French in the Cathedral of Notre-Dame in Paris, in the presence of the Pope. France, fifteen years after the outbreak of the Revolution and twelve years since the proclamation of the Republic, thus became an empire. Four days later, on 18 May, the Consular Guard received its new denomination of Imperial Guard. This change did not affect the internal structure of the Foot Grenadiers, the senior regiment of the Imperial Guard's infantry. These were the direct heirs of the Guard of the Executive Directorate that had been organized during 1796, and comprised two companies of foot grenadiers with 120 men each. These were, from the outset, hand-picked veterans with certain special characteristics: they were all literate, they had to be at least 1.8 metres tall, they had to have perfect personal records and they had to have combat experience in at least two campaigns. To ensure their loyalty, the government gave them the same pay as the corporals of the line infantry units. When the Guard of the Directorate was absorbed into the Consular Guard, command of the unit was given to Joachim Murat, who was one of Napoleon's most loyal and capable generals. Murat did his best to transform the new Consular Guard into a model unit for the rest of the French Army, selecting potential members in a very rigid way fashion. Admission to the unit was restricted only to those veterans who had performed heroic actions or had given proof of exemplary conduct, while soldiers aged under 25 could not serve in the Guard. Robust constitution was another requirement, together with a height of between 1.78 and 1.84 metres. Like the former members of the Guard of the Directorate, the new guardsmen had to be literate and were required to have combat experience, this time in at least three campaigns. The Foot Grenadiers were the 'elite of the elite' inside the Consular Guard, thanks to their strict discipline and imposing appearance. Many of them had followed Napoleon since his first campaign of 1796, and all of them were extremely loyal to the First Consul. In exchange for their services, the guardsmen received elegant uniforms and good food, enjoying much better living conditions compared with the ordinary soldiers of the line units. A member of the Foot Grenadiers received a standard pay that was almost twice that of an ordinary fusilier, this preferential economic treatment being a status symbol for all members of the Guard.

The Foot Grenadiers and Foot Chasseurs   17

Sergeant of the Foot Grenadiers.

In 1802, the staff of the Foot Grenadiers comprised the following elements: one chef de brigade, two chefs de bataillon, two capitaines, one quartier-maitre, two adjutants, two porte-drapeaux, two surgeons, one drum-major, two drum-corporals, one chef de musique and forty-eight musicians. The sixteen companies of the corps each had 110 NCOs/privates. Until November 1801, there had been twelve companies, always in two battalions. During Napoleon's second Italian campaign, the Foot Grenadiers fought for the first time as a unit at the bloody Battle of Marengo. Here they stood firm during the most decisive moment of the clash, gaining a new nickname for their corps, the 'fortress of granite'. After the victory at Marengo, the Consular Guard was greatly expanded. The initial single company of Foot Chasseurs, whose members had been part of the Guides of Bonaparte, was gradually enlarged and finally became a regiment, having the same internal composition as the Foot Grenadiers (albeit with only thirty-five musicians instead of forty-eight). The required height to be part of the Foot Chasseurs was 1.7 metres and not 1.8 metres like for the Foot Grenadiers; despite this, the two units soon started to be very similar, and their members always had the same military status. As previously mentioned, in 1804, Napoleon decided to create a corps of potential officers/cadets to be attached to the foot regiments of the Consular Guard. Since the aristocratic word 'cadets' could not be included in the official

Soldier (left) and officers (right) of the Foot Grenadiers.

denomination of a military unit serving the French Republic, the First Consul suggested using the Latin term '*velites*' to designate the new corps. These, as explained above, comprised two battalions with five companies each that were attached to the Foot Grenadiers and Foot Chasseurs; the first was known as Vélite-Grenadiers and the second as Vélite-Chasseurs. Officers and NCOs of these two battalions were drawn from the Foot Grenadiers and Foot Chasseurs, while privates were all young recruits (with little experience) from the most prominent families of France. To become part of the Velites, a recruit had to pay 200 francs.

From 1806, the whole Imperial Guard, as we will see in the following chapters, was greatly expanded thanks to the formation of several new units. As a result, in order to differentiate the various corps according to their experience, the units of the Guard were later assembled into three groups: the Old Guard, the Middle Guard and the Young Guard. The Old Guard was formed from the veteran corps that already existed before 1805 and whose soldiers had followed Napoleon since his first military campaigns of 1796/97. The Middle Guard was formed of younger veterans, who fought under Napoleon's orders during the first victorious campaigns of the Empire (1805–09). The Young Guard comprised units that were organized after 1809, and whose members were young recruits; these were the best and fittest elements chosen from the annual intake of conscripts and volunteers who were recruited for service in the French Army. The Foot Grenadiers and Foot Chasseurs, together with their attached corps of Velites, represented the core of the Old Guard's infantry. When the Imperial Guard was officially created, the Foot Grenadiers had the following regimental staff: one colonel, one major, three chefs de bataillon, three adjutant-majors, three assistants, two porte-drapeaux, three medical officers, one drum-major, three drum-corporals, one chef de musique and forty-six musicians. The single companies of the two battalions included the following elements: one captain, one first-lieutenant, two second-lieutenants, one sergeant-major, four sergeants, one quartermaster-corporal, eight corporals, two sappers, two drummers and eighty grenadiers. The single companies of Vélite-Grenadiers had one captain, one first-lieutenant, one second-lieutenant, one sergeant-major, four sergeants, one quartermaster-corporal, eight corporals, one drummer and 172 velites. The Foot Chasseurs had the same internal organization as the Foot Grenadiers, while the Vélite-Chasseurs had the same composition as the Vélite-Grenadiers.

During the 1805 campaign, which culminated with victory over Russia and Austria at the Battle of Austerlitz, neither the Foot Grenadiers nor the Foot Chasseurs took part in any significant action. By that time, however, they already had a legendary reputation. The Foot Grenadiers, in particular, were the best heavy infantry soldiers in the whole French Army: they were known as the '*grognards*' (the 'grumblers') because they used to complain in the presence of the emperor and enjoyed a special personal relationship with him. They were older and battle-hardened fighters who had followed Napoleon since 1796 and were extremely loyal to him. Bonaparte was nicknamed 'the little corporal' by his Foot Grenadiers, who were all much taller than him. Napoleon loved his guardsmen, and his guardsmen loved him. The emperor always took great care of his Guard and gave many privileges to his veterans. Members of the Imperial Guard, as we have seen above, were paid much more than the soldiers of ordinary units and enjoyed a better daily life: they received excellent rations, had the best equipment, lived in the most comfortable quarters and ranked one grade higher than all non-Imperial Guard French soldiers. From a uniform point of view, the Foot Grenadiers and Foot Chasseurs could be easily distinguished from all other infantry units thanks to the fact that they wore massive bearskins. In addition, they had the privilege of being employed in battle only when strictly needed (as the events of Austerlitz had demonstrated). They were the best of the best, thanks to their superior training and combat experience, with unrivalled determination and morale. In essence, the Imperial Guard was a tactical reserve, which was used by Napoleon only when it appeared a battle was going to be lost. During the 1806 campaign in Prussia, the infantry of the Old Guard was kept in reserve and thus did not play any significant part in the Battle of Jena, but the *grognards* finally had the opportunity to distinguish themselves in a major pitched clash during the following year. The occasion came during the Battle of Eylau, a bloody two-day clash between the French under Napoleon and a Russian army (supported by some Prussian military units). The emperor came very near to defeat at Eylau, and at one point, to stabilize a dangerous situation, he was forced to order a frontal bayonet charge by his Old Guard. This, together with the arrival of French reinforcements, changed the outcome of the clash in favour of Napoleon, although the battle ultimately proved inconclusive. During the ensuing Battle of Friedland, which brought the 1807 Polish campaign to an end in Napoleon's favour, the Foot Grenadiers and Foot Chasseurs were again kept in reserve. They complained very frequently about this, being loyal to their nickname of 'grumblers'.

Napoleon decided to expand the infantry of the Imperial Guard in 1806, ordering all line infantry battalions of the French Army to send one of their best soldiers to the Guard in order to have a good number of new veterans. The men sent by the line battalions had to be under 35 years of age and have a good conduct record comprising at least one citation of valour over ten years of service. On 15 April 1806, with the arrival of these new soldiers, it was possible to create the following new units: 2nd Regiment of Foot Grenadiers, 2nd Regiment of Foot Chasseurs, 2nd Battalion of Vélite-Grenadiers and 2nd Battalion of Vélite-Chasseurs. During September 1806,

The Foot Grenadiers and Foot Chasseurs 21

Officer (left), sergeant-major (centre) and soldiers (right) of the Foot Grenadiers.

the Velites of the Imperial Guard were completely reorganized: the 1st Battalion of Vélite-Grenadiers and the 1st Battalion of Vélite-Chasseurs were combined to form an independent Regiment of Velites, with two battalions of four companies each. The 2nd Battalion of Vélite-Grenadiers and the 2nd Battalion of Vélite-Chasseurs, meanwhile, were melded in order to create a new Regiment of Fusiliers (with two battalions of four companies each). A few months after these changes, the Regiment of Velites was renamed the 2nd Regiment of Fusiliers and the original Regiment of Fusiliers was renamed the 1st Regiment of Fusiliers. As a result, the velites disappeared from the establishment of the Imperial Guard and their members lost their original 'cadet' character. The two new units of fusiliers were also known, respectively, as the Fusiliers-Grenadiers and the Fusiliers-Chasseurs. Over time, they started to be made up of picked recruits and not of young potential officers from the richest families of France. The new regiments of fusiliers never had the same special status as the Foot Grenadiers and Foot Chasseurs, since they were not made up of battle-hardened veterans. As a result, they were not part of the Old Guard but of the Middle Guard. This was also clearly visible from their uniforms, which included as headgear a simple bicorn and not the massive bearskin of the Old Guard.

In 1809, after a period of relative peace, Napoleon decided to reduce the number of the Old Guard's foot regiments. The 1st Foot Grenadiers and 2nd Foot Grenadiers were combined into a single Regiment of Foot Grenadiers, while the 1st Foot Chasseurs joined with the 2nd Foot Chasseurs to form the Regiment of Foot Chasseurs. Each of the two consolidated units had two battalions with four companies, each of which had a higher number of men than previously. The Imperial Guard had great economic costs and so, by consolidating units, the emperor hoped to reduce them in a sensible way. On 13 September 1810, the infantry of the Old Guard absorbed a new unit which had previously been part of the Dutch Royal Guard. In 1795, during the Revolutionary Wars, the Netherlands had been invaded by the French and their government had been deposed. The country was thereafter transformed into the Batavian Republic, a satellite of Republican France, and sent its military forces to fight alongside the French during the following years. In 1806, Napoleon decided to transform the Batavian Republic into the new Kingdom of Holland, which remained a protectorate of France and was ruled by Louis Bonaparte, brother of the emperor, who was crowned King of Holland. After assuming power, Louis organized a strong Royal Guard that was modelled on Napoleon's Imperial Guard. During the following years, however, he demonstrated his inability to govern the Netherlands, failing to achieve any of the objectives that Napoleon had given him. As a result, in 1810, the emperor decided to absorb the Kingdom of Holland into the French Empire and to remove his inept brother from the throne. The best

The Foot Grenadiers and Foot Chasseurs 23

Soldier of the Foot Grenadiers.

units of the Dutch Royal Guard were incorporated into the French Imperial Guard; these included an elite regiment of grenadiers, which became part of the Imperial Guard as the 2nd Regiment of Foot Grenadiers. They kept their former uniforms, which included a massive bearskin like those of the French *grognards*, but which were white instead of dark blue. As a result, these 'Dutch Grenadiers' were always easily recognizable from the other corps of the Imperial Guard. As we will see, this was just one of the many foreign units that were part of Napoleon's Imperial Guard. At the time of its inclusion into the French Army, the regiment comprised the following elements: forty-six officers, 1,188 NCOs/soldiers, sixteen sappers, forty musicians and 150 velites (cadets).

The Dutch Royal Guard also comprised a company of veteran soldiers, who were no longer fit for active military service but could be employed to perform garrison duties. These guarded the royal palace of Louis Bonaparte until 1810, when, like the Dutch Grenadiers, they were absorbed into the Imperial Guard. The Imperial Guard already had a company of veterans, which had originally been created as part of the Consular Guard and which continued to exist until 1815. The Dutch Royal Guard also included a Garde du Corps, or Bodyguard, which was disbanded in 1810: some of its members were absorbed into the units of the French Old Guard and others were attached to the Dutch Grenadiers (the 150 velites of this unit). It became increasingly difficult for Napoleon to find old veterans who could serve in the Foot Grenadiers and in the Foot Chasseurs. At the beginning of 1811, for example, there were only 530 soldiers of the Old Guard who had served under him in Italy or in Egypt. Despite this, on 18 May 1811, the Emperor decided to enlarge the infantry of the Imperial Guard by forming two new regiments: the 2nd Regiment of Foot Grenadiers and the 2nd Regiment of Foot Chasseurs. These units had already existed before 1809, as we have seen above, so the Dutch Grenadiers, who had become part of the French Army only in 1810, became the 3rd Regiment of Foot Grenadiers and lost their original denomination of the 2nd Regiment.

Napoleon launched his ill-fated invasion of Russia in 1812, assembling his Grande Armée of over 600,000 soldiers. These included the entire Imperial Guard, which was organized as an army corps that included several divisions. One of these, the 3rd Division, comprised the five foot regiments described above: the 1st, 2nd and 3rd Foot Grenadiers and the 1st and 2nd Foot Chasseurs. The first three units were assembled into a 'grenadier brigade', the remaining two making up a 'chasseur brigade'. At the Battle of Borodino, the largest clash of the Russian campaign, Napoleon decided not to employ his Old Guard, keeping it in reserve. It is likely that, if he had have risked the life of his loyal veterans in battle, the emperor could have achieved a decisive victory over the Russians. During the long and terrible retreat that followed the

The Foot Grenadiers and Foot Chasseurs 25

Soldier of the Foot Grenadiers with the dark blue trousers worn during winter.

French occupation of Moscow, the infantry of the Old Guard fought with great courage on several occasions while protecting their emperor. Like all other units of the Grande Armée, they suffered huge casualties.

The Russian campaign practically destroyed the infantry of the Old Guard. By the time the retreat ended, the five regiments were reduced to the following strengths: the 1st Foot Grenadiers had thirty-eight officers and 369 men; the 2nd Foot Grenadiers thirty-nine officers and 234 men; the 3rd Foot Grenadiers twenty-four officers and just seventeen men; the 1st Foot Chasseurs twenty-eight officers and 435 men; and the 2nd Foot Chasseurs thirty officers and 257 men. The Emperor did his best to rebuild the devastated units of the Old Guard during 1813, but although they were restored to their previous establishments, their members were no longer of the same quality as the old *grognards*. The Dutch Grenadiers, due to the particularly terrible losses suffered, were not re-formed after the Russian campaign. During the 1813 campaign in Germany and that in France in 1814, the Imperial Guard fought with great courage and participated in several actions, but it could do little to prevent the invasion of France and the fall of the Empire. By April 1814, with the Allies closing in on final victory, the regiments of Foot Grenadiers mustered a total of 1,360 survivors and the Foot Chasseurs just 1,296. The *grognards* wished to end their careers by fighting one last desperate battle in the streets of Paris, but their emperor prevented them from doing so and ordered them to surrender like the rest of the French Army. After being forced to abdicate, Napoleon was permitted to retain a personal guard of just 1,000 men who followed him into exile on the isle of Elba. The emperor chose these soldiers from his beloved veterans of the Old Guard, some of whom had been fighting with him since 1796. The 1,000 guardsmen were assembled into a single battalion, which was Napoleon's 'personal army'. Before leaving France for Elba, the emperor decided to meet the veterans of his Old Guard for the last time at Fontainebleau. Here Napoleon paid a tearful farewell to his 'grumblers', with a dramatic speech that ended with the following words: 'I cannot embrace you all, but I shall embrace your general.' After kissing the colours of the 1st Foot Grenadiers, the emperor left Fontainebleau and went into exile.

With the restoration of monarchy in France, the former members of the Imperial Guard were absorbed into the recreated Royal Guard. This corps comprised one Regiment of Royal Grenadiers and one Regiment of Royal Chasseurs, which had three battalions each. These new units, however, were never loyal to the restored monarchy, continuing their Bonapartist associations. In 1815, Napoleon returned to France after less than a year of exile. He landed in southern France at the head of the 1,000 veterans who had shared his exile on Elba. Louis XVIII, the new King of France, ordered his army to capture Napoleon as soon as possible, but within a

The Foot Grenadiers and Foot Chasseurs 27

Corporal of the Foot Grenadiers with the bicorn and *surtout* worn on campaign.

Veteran of the Foot Grenadiers with the dark blue greatcoat worn during winter.

few days, all the units sent to apprehend the emperor joined him in his advance on Paris. Louis had no choice but to abandon France. Unsurprisingly, the Regiment of Royal Grenadiers and the Regiment of Royal Chasseurs were among the first corps to abandon the restored monarchy. After these events, Napoleon reorganized his Imperial Guard in view of the new military campaigns that he knew would have to be fought. Eight new regiments of infantry were created: four of Foot Grenadiers and four of Foot Chasseurs. It should be noted, however, that only a very small percentage of soldiers from these units were actual veterans; by now the majority were simple young recruits, not so different from those of the line infantry regiments. New 3rd Regiments were created on 8 April 1815, quickly followed by new 4th Regiments on 9 May. The elite 'Elba Battalion' was included in the 1st Regiment of Foot Grenadiers, the only corps of the Old Guard that was still made up of *vieux moustaches* ('old moustaches', another nickname of the guardsmen). The new 3rd and 4th Regiments were not units of great quality, since they were not equipped properly and constantly lacked the necessary men to fill the establishments prescribed on paper.

During the climactic Battle of Waterloo on 18 June 1815, the Old Guard was initially kept in reserve, but when the French seemed to be on the verge of victory, Napoleon decided to employ his veterans in order to break the Duke of Wellington's Anglo-Belgian lines. The guardsmen launched a frontal bayonet assault, which came

Members of the Foot Grenadiers, including standard-bearer, drummer, drum-major and sapper.

near to success; in the end, however, the attack was repulsed by the Foot Guards of the British Army, who delivered terrible fire upon the French infantrymen. The famous cry '*La Garde recule*' ('The Guard is falling back') spread terror among the ranks of Napoleon's army and made clear that the battle had been lost. The 1st Foot Grenadiers, who had still been kept in reserve during the failed assault, tried to hold their ground and stem the flow of fugitives from other units. The Old Guard, as on previous occasions, remained loyal to its motto 'The Guard dies but does not surrender'. Surrounded by the enemy, the Foot Grenadiers formed a defensive square (with Napoleon in the centre) and marched away from the battlefield in close formation. With the second exile and definitive fall of Napoleon, all the foot regiments of the Imperial Guard were disbanded during in September and October 1815. At Waterloo they had written the last page of glory in their bloody history, which had commenced sixteen years before. In world history, no military unit had ever been so loyal for so long to a single man as the *grognards* were to their 'little corporal'.

Uniforms and equipment

The early Guard of the Legislative Corps, created in 1791, wore the same uniform of the royal Garde de la Prevote from which it had been formed. This comprised the following elements: black tricorn edged in gold with black-and-white cockade; dark blue coat with red folded collar and round cuffs, golden lace to collar and cuffs, and additional golden lace on the frontal buttonholes of the coat; red waistcoat with edges and horizontal pockets piped in gold; red breeches and stockings; light blue-and-golden crossbelt with black leather ammunition pouch; and black shoes. The Grenadier Corps of the National Gendarmerie adopted the same uniform as the new National Gendarmerie: black bearskin with red cords and plume; dark blue tunic with red collar and round cuffs (piped in white), red frontal lapels with white piping to external edges and buttonholes, and white *contre-épaulettes* (i.e. fringeless epaulettes); buff colour waistcoat and trousers; black leggings and shoes; and buff leather belt equipment. This uniform was partly modified at a later date: the collar became red and the white *contre-épaulettes* were replaced by red epaulettes. The white piping on the buttonholes of the lapels was removed, while white cuff flaps were added. All the other elements remained the same. When the Guard of the Legislative Corps was reformed, it received a new and much simpler dress that resembled that of the National Guard: black bearskin with white metal frontal plate and red plume; dark blue tunic with dark blue collar, red round cuffs piped in white and white cuff flaps, red epaulettes on the shoulders and red frontal lapels piped in white; white waistcoat and trousers; black leggings and shoes; and white leather belt equipment. The Guard of the Executive Directorate, created in 1796, already had the uniform that would later become the standard dress of the Imperial Guard's Foot Grenadiers: black bearskin with brass frontal plate, red cords and plume; dark blue coat with red collar and round cuffs, red epaulettes, white frontal lapels and cuff flaps; white waistcoat, trousers and leggings; black shoes; and white leather belt equipment. This dress, like that of the National Guard and Guard of the Legislative Corps, included the three colours of France's new national flag. The Foot Grenadiers of the Consular Guard, organized by Napoleon in 1799, were dressed quite similarly to those protecting the members of the Directorate: black bearskin with brass frontal plate, white cords and red plume; dark blue tunic with dark blue collar and red round cuffs, red epaulettes and white frontal lapels; white waistcoat, trousers and leggings; black shoes; and white leather belt equipment. The brass plate on the front of the bearskin was decorated with a flaming grenade and the inscription 'GARDE DES CONSULS;. The Foot Chasseurs of the Consular Guard were dressed similarly: black bearskin without frontal plate but with white cords and red-and-green plume; dark blue tunic with dark blue collar and red pointed cuffs (piped in white), red epaulettes with green 'crescents' and white frontal lapels; white waistcoat, trousers and leggings; black shoes; and white leather belt equipment. As is clear from the above description, green was the distinctive colour of the Foot Chasseurs.

When the Consular Guard was transformed into the Imperial Guard, the uniform of the Foot Grenadiers did not change in any significant way: black bearskin with brass frontal plate (showing an Imperial Eagle), white cords and red plume; dark blue tunic with dark blue collar and red round cuffs, red epaulettes on the shoulders, white cuff flaps and white frontal lapels; white waistcoat, trousers and leggings; black shoes; and white leather belt equipment. Rank was shown by yellow stripes (piped in red) that were applied on the tunic's sleeves just above the cuffs; 'V'-shaped *chevrons* (yellow stripes piped in red), applied on the upper part of the sleeves, showed the years of service of each individual. The Foot Chasseurs were dressed similarly to the Foot Grenadiers, albeit with some peculiarities: black bearskin without frontal plate but having white cords and red-and-green plume; dark blue tunic with dark blue collar and red pointed cuffs (piped in white), green epaulettes with red 'crescents' on the shoulders and white frontal lapels; white waistcoat, trousers and leggings; black shoes; and white leather belt equipment. These uniforms were worn by all the units of Foot Grenadiers and Foot Chasseurs that were part of the Imperial Guard, except for the Dutch Grenadiers. The latter retained their distinctive uniform after being absorbed into the French Army, which included the following elements: black bearskin without frontal plate but with white cords and red plume; white tunic with

The regimental band of the Foot Grenadiers.

red collar and red round cuffs, red epaulettes on the shoulders, white cuff flaps and red frontal lapels; white waistcoat, trousers and leggings; black shoes; and white leather belt equipment.

The Vélite-Grenadiers and Vélite-Chasseurs were dressed as follows: black bicorn with French national cockade and coloured plume (entirely red for the Vélite-Grenadiers, red-and-green for the Vélite-Chasseurs); dark blue tunic with dark blue collar piped in red and red round cuffs piped in white, dark blue shoulder straps

Sergeant (left) and soldier (right) of the Foot Chasseurs.

piped in red, dark blue cuff flaps piped in white and white frontal lapels; white waistcoat, trousers and leggings; black shoes; and white leather belt equipment. Both the Foot Grenadiers and the Foot Chasseurs included a certain number of sappers, elite combat engineers who performed a series of fundamental functions inside their units. They were tasked with removing all the obstacles that could be encountered by their regiment during a march, and were also charged with the construction of field fortifications during pitched battles. Due to their specific functions, they wore some peculiar pieces of equipment, including a pair of white leather gloves and a large white leather apron. Their main working tool was a massive axe, which was their mark of distinction together with their long beards. The sappers also had their own distinctive badge, consisting of two crossed axes, which was embroidered on the sleeves of their tunic and also applied on the front of their white crossbelts. The personal equipment of each Foot Grenadier and each Foot Chasseur included two crossbelts: one held the black leather ammunition pouch, the other the black leather bayonet scabbard as well as the black leather scabbard of the infantry short sword (*sabre-briquet*). Each soldier had a brown knapsack with white leather slings, which was carried on the back with the rolled greatcoat on top. The dark blue greatcoat was double-breasted and was used only during winter. It was particularly popular on campaign and had some elements in common with the tunic: epaulettes on the shoulders and rank/seniority stripes on the sleeves.

In addition to the uniforms described in the previous paragraphs, the soldiers of the Foot Grenadiers and the Foot Chasseurs also had a simpler campaign dress that was worn on most occasions during ordinary service. This did not feature a standard tunic with frontal lapels but a single-breasted frock coat known as a *surtout*. This was entirely dark blue, including collar and round cuffs, but had the same epaulettes as the ordinary tunic. On campaign, the *surtout* was frequently worn together with dark blue trousers, which were particularly popular during winter months. With the campaign dress comprising *surtout* and dark blue trousers, the Foot Grenadiers and Foot Chasseurs frequently wore a black bicorn instead of the massive and uncomfortable bearskin. The bicorn had a French national cockade on the front and a small plume (entirely red for Foot Grenadiers, red-and-green for Foot Chasseurs); in addition, it had four extra stripes of coloured lace on the front (in the same colour as the small plume). Like all the French infantrymen, the soldiers of the Old Guard also had a fatigue cap – used inside the barracks – that was known as a *bonnet de police*. This was dark blue with red piping and frontal tassel. The Dutch Grenadiers had their own campaign uniform: black bicorn with national cockade, red plume and red stripes of coloured lace; white *surtout* with red collar and white round cuffs (piped in red), red piping to the front and bottom edges of the *surtout* and red epaulettes on the shoulders; white

The Foot Grenadiers and Foot Chasseurs 35

Sappers of the Foot Chasseurs.

trousers; black leggings; and black shoes. The musicians of each regiment, like the sappers, had their own peculiar dress, that was usually characterized by the presence of extravagant decorations. A standard company drummer wore the same uniform as the other soldiers, but with additional golden lace on the collar and cuffs of the tunic,

as well as on the external edges and buttonholes of the frontal lapels. The musicians of the Dutch Grenadiers were an exception to this general rule, since they were dressed in light blue with yellow facings and not in white with red facings like the rest of their regiment. Their additional lace was not golden but silver. The musicians of the regimental staff had much more ornate uniforms than those described above, characterized by a profusion of additional golden lace on all garments. Decorative golden knots were embroidered on the frontal part of the trousers, and headgear consisted of a black bicorn decorated with feathers (in the national colours of France). Officers of the Foot Grenadiers and Foot Chasseurs wore the same uniforms as their men, but their rank was shown by golden epaulettes and *contre-épaulettes* positioned on the shoulders; in addition, they had a brass gorget (crescent-shaped plate) on the chest as a mark of distinction.

Sapper of the Foot Chasseurs.

Chapter 3

The Infantry of the Middle Guard and Young Guard

History and organization

The Foot Grenadiers and Foot Chasseurs were without doubt the most famous foot units of the Imperial Guard, but from 1806, they started to be supplemented by several new infantry corps that were part of the Middle Guard and the Young Guard. These units did not consist of battle-hardened veterans like those of the Old Guard, but contributed significantly to the war effort of Napoleonic France. Differently from the Foot Grenadiers and Foot Chasseurs, they were employed quite frequently during pitched battles. The infantry corps of the Middle Guard were the Regiment of Fusiliers-Grenadiers and the Regiment of Fusiliers-Chasseurs. These, as we have seen in the previous chapter, were created on 19 October 1806 by assembling together and transforming the battalions of Velites that were attached to the infantry of the Old Guard. Both units consisted of two battalions, with four companies each until 5 January 1811, when a fifth company was added to each battalion. The battalions of Fusiliers-Grenadiers and Fusiliers-Chasseurs were further enlarged in December 1813 with the addition of a sixth company. Since their formation, the two regiments of Fusiliers had lost the 'cadet' character of the previous Velites battalions; in addition, the majority of their members started to be normal recruits from the reserve companies of the various French departments rather than young gentlemen wishing to initiate a military career. During their regimental history, the Fusiliers-Grenadiers and Fusiliers-Chasseurs always worked as a kind of generational link between the corps of the Old Guard and those of the Young Guard (which were formed after 1809). In addition, they always remained strongly linked to the corps to which they had been previously attached (the Foot Grenadiers for the Fusiliers-Grenadiers and the Foot Chasseurs for the Fusiliers-Chasseurs). In 1809, when he decided to reduce the economic costs deriving from the Imperial Guard, Napoleon preferred disbanding the 2nd Regiment of Foot Grenadiers and 2nd Regiment of Foot Chasseurs instead of the two Fusilier regiments because the latter cost much less. During the same year, the emperor also decided to expand the infantry of his Guard by creating several new corps, which would make up the new Young Guard.

The first of these new units was the Tirailleurs-Grenadiers, formed on 16 January 1809. The term 'Tirailleurs', which means 'skirmishers' in French, was introduced by Napoleon to designate the members of the new infantry units created inside his Young Guard. These were all conscripts and not picked veterans, so they needed to have a new specific title. 'Tirailleurs' worked well in this sense, since it was not offensive for the veterans of the Old Guard nor derogatory for the new soldiers. As clear from the name, they were equipped and trained as light infantry. The new regiment was attached to the Foot Grenadiers of the Old Guard, hence its complete denomination of Tirailleurs-Grenadiers. It consisted of two battalions, with six companies each; officers and NCOs were taken from the ranks of the Old Guard. Consequently, the new corps had a lot in common with the previous Vélite-Grenadiers. On 29 March 1809, another two foot units were added to the Imperial Guard: the Tirailleurs-Chasseurs and Conscripts-Grenadiers. The former was very similar to the Tirailleurs-Grenadiers but was attached to the Foot Chasseurs, while the latter was attached to the Foot Grenadiers and consisted entirely of younger conscripts (hence the unit's name). Both regiments, like that formed a few weeks before, comprised two battalions with six companies each. They were followed on 31 March 1809 by another three new regiments of the Young Guard: the 2nd Conscripts-Grenadiers, 1st Conscripts-Chasseurs and 2nd Conscripts-Chasseurs. Although Napoleon was expanding his Imperial Guard by forming new units, these were only of the same quality as those of the line infantry; his hope was that they could improve by serving alongside the veterans of the Old Guard. On 25 April 1809, this general expansion temporarily came to an end with the creation of another two regiments: the 2nd Tirailleurs-Grenadiers and 2nd Tirailleurs-Chasseurs.

After all these changes, the infantry of the Young Guard consisted of the following corps: 1st Regiment of Tirailleurs-Grenadiers, 2nd Regiment of Tirailleurs-Grenadiers, 1st Regiment of Tirailleurs-Chasseurs, 2nd Regiment of Tirailleurs-Chasseurs, 1st Regiment of Conscripts-Grenadiers, 2nd Regiment of Conscripts-Grenadiers, 1st Regiment of Conscripts-Chasseurs and 2nd Regiment of Conscripts-Chasseurs. In just a few months, during the first half of 1809, eight new regiments had been created. These were mostly made up of conscripts from the classes of 1808–09, who had no military experience at all. Officers and NCOs for the four Tirailleur regiments mostly came from the two units of the Old Guard that had recently been disbanded: the 2nd Foot Grenadiers and 2nd Foot Chasseurs. After two years of service in the Tirailleur units, a soldier could be admitted into the Fusilier corps of the Middle Guard; after four years' service in the latter, he could be assigned to the infantry of the Old Guard but only by virtue of an Imperial decree. In the hierarchy of the Imperial Guard, the Tirailleurs were superior to the Conscripts, who

The Infantry of the Middle Guard and Young Guard 39

Soldier of the Dutch Grenadiers.

were also equipped as light infantry but received the same standard of pay as the line infantry. The officers of the Conscripts came from the Old Guard, while the NCOs came from the Middle Guard.

During March 1809, the Young Guard had also been enlarged with the creation of another two small units which were not recruited in France. Napoleon had dominated most of the Italian peninsula since 1796, and in 1805, after becoming Emperor of the French, he was also crowned King of Italy in Milan. Since that year, most of northern and central Italy was organized into a new state known as Regno Italico, which was France's most loyal ally during the Napoleonic era. Not all the regions of northern and central Italy, however, were part of the Kingdom of Italy. There were two that had been directly annexed to the French Empire during previous years: Piedmont and Tuscany. As a result, in 1809, Napoleon decided to raise two new units of Velites in these Italian territories of France. The emperor thereby wished to reinforce his personal links with the most prominent families of his Italian territories by creating new cadet corps, in whose ranks young gentlemen could initiate their military career. Each member of the new corps, in exchange for the privilege of becoming a Velite, was paid a sum of

200 francs per annum. The Velites of Turin, 475-strong, were initially recruited as the bodyguard of Napoleon's brother-in-law Prince Borghese, who was governor of the Trans-Alpine Departments of the French Empire, comprising Piedmont. The Velites of Florence, 600-strong, were originally raised as the bodyguard of Napoleon's

Soldier of the Dutch Grenadiers (left) and of the 1st Battalion of Pupilles (right).

sister Elisa, who was at the head (albeit only formally) of Tuscany. Both units were battalions and not regiments.

In 1809, while Napoleon and his Imperial Guard were fighting in Central Europe against Austria, the British landed an expeditionary corps at Walcheren in the Netherlands. Louis Bonaparte, as King of Holland, was charged with contesting the British invasion, but from the beginning of operations he demonstrated mediocre military command skills. His forces reacted very slowly to the attack, and there was a strong risk that the British could thereby open a second front in Europe. These events would lead to the abdication of Louis as King of Holland and the incorporation of the Netherlands into the French Empire. Since Napoleon was fighting with his Grande Armée against the Austrians, he had no choice but to mobilize National Guard units from the departments of northern France and send them against the British, with Marshal Bernadotte as supreme commander. Against the odds, the National Guardsmen were able to obtain a series of successes against the invaders and the British were eventually expelled from Walcheren. The emperor, pleasantly surprised by the courage and competence with which his National Guardsmen had fought, decided to absorb the best of them into his regular forces. Consequently, in January 1810, Napoleon ordered the establishment of a new infantry regiment of the Young Guard made up of National Guardsmen from northern France. Initially, the new unit had four battalions with four companies each, but it was quickly reduced to two battalions with six companies each on 29 May 1810.

In December 1810, in order to distinguish the Tirailleurs attached to the Foot Grenadiers from those attached to the Foot Chasseurs, the latter received the new denomination of Voltigeurs. As a result, the four units of Tirailleurs received the following new titles: 1st and 2nd Regiment of Tirailleurs for those attached to the Foot Grenadiers; and 1st and 2nd Regiment of Voltigeurs for those attached to the Foot Chasseurs. In February 1811, the 1st and 2nd Regiment of Conscripts-Grenadiers were redesignated as the 3rd and 4th Regiment of Tirailleurs; at the same time, the 1st and 2nd Regiment of Conscripts-Chasseurs became the 3rd and 4th Regiment of Voltigeurs. As we have seen, the Kingdom of Holland was absorbed into the French Empire in 1810 and its Royal Guard was made part of the Imperial Guard. At the time of its disbandment, the Dutch Royal Guard included a corps of young cadets who were all orphans and whose fathers had died while serving in the Dutch Army. When these Dutch Velites were transferred to the French Army, Napoleon was particularly impressed by their discipline and personal determination. He therefore decided that his Imperial Guard should also comprise a military unit made up of war orphans. These were trained as Imperial Guardsmen of the future, and were seen as 'sons of the emperor'. The new corps received the denomination of

Soldier of the Fusiliers-Grenadiers.

The Infantry of the Middle Guard and Young Guard 43

Soldier of the Fusiliers-Grenadiers.

Pupilles of the Imperial Guard, whose members, as well as all being orphans of war, included some of the cadets from the Kingdom of Holland. By August 1811, the Pupilles were already the largest regiment of the Imperial Guard, with an impressive establishment of eight active battalions and one depot battalion. They were, however, only a training unit and could not be used to fight like the other corps of the Guard. Each battalion comprised 800 Pupilles (i.e. boys), and thus the whole regiment had a total of 8,000 members (who came not only from France, but also from other territories controlled by Napoleon). According to the emperor's plans, the Pupilles would enter the ranks of combat units upon reaching the age of 18, and thus would form a nucleus of well-trained young soldiers. This system, however, could never work properly because the French Empire was defeated before most of the Pupilles could be transferred to the combat corps of the Imperial Guard.

In May 1811, Napoleon continued expanding the infantry of his Young Guard, creating a 5th Regiment of Tirailleurs and 5th Regiment of Voltigeurs, these being followed within a few weeks by a 6th Regiment of Tirailleurs and 6th Regiment of Voltigeurs. The emperor, however, was well aware that the various foot units of the Young Guard were of no great quality and that, despite their official denominations, they did not have the basic characteristics that were typical of light infantry. For these reasons, he decided to create a new regiment to be trained and equipped as proper elite light infantry. This unit was recruited from the sons or nephews of the foresters guarding the Imperial or public forests of France. Napoleon needed new recruits who could operate effectively on broken terrain to conduct reconnaissance missions or to attack a superior enemy by using hit-and-run tactics. His Imperial Guard lacked a proper light infantry corps, and thus was not capable of operating in areas covered with dense woods. As forests were quite common in Central Europe, the Emperor desperately needed a new unit that could move rapidly on every kind of terrain. This corps, formed in September 1811, received the denomination of 'Flanqueurs', a term indicating those light skirmishers who operated on the flanks of the line infantry formations. After five years of service in the new regiment, the Flanqueurs could succeed to their father's or uncle's posts and leave the Imperial Guard. The structure of the corps comprised two battalions with six companies each, like in most other regiments from the Young Guard. During 1811, Napoleon also created an independent Bataillon d'Instruction, or Training Battalion, inside the Imperial Guard, which was garrisoned in Fontainebleau and was charged with training future NCOs of the Young Guard. This was later increased to an establishment of four battalions.

As is clear from the above, within a few years the Imperial Guard was greatly expanded by Napoleon, to such an extent that by the outbreak of the Russian campaign in 1812, it had the numerical consistency of an army corps. For the invasion of Russia, the infantry units of the Guard were grouped into three divisions as follows:

The Infantry of the Middle Guard and Young Guard 45

Soldier of the Fusiliers-Grenadiers (left) and of the Tirailleurs-Grenadiers (right).

1st Division
  1st Brigade
  4th Regiment of Tirailleurs
  1st Regiment of Voltigeurs
  5th Regiment of Voltigeurs

  2nd Brigade
  5th Regiment of Tirailleurs
  6th Regiment of Tirailleurs
  6th Regiment of Voltigeurs

2nd Division
  1st Brigade
  1st Regiment of Tirailleurs
  1st Regiment of Voltigeurs

  2nd Brigade
  Regiment of Fusiliers-Grenadiers
  Regiment of Fusiliers-Chasseurs
  Regiment of Flanqueurs

3rd Division
  1st Brigade
  1st Regiment of Foot Chasseurs
  2nd Regiment of Foot Chasseurs

  2nd Brigade
  1st Regiment of Foot Grenadiers
  2nd Regiment of Foot Grenadiers
  3rd Regiment of Foot Grenadiers

The infantry of the Imperial Guard fought with enormous courage during the retreat from Russia, saving the rest of the French Army from total destruction on several occasions. By the end of the 1812 campaign, however, very little remained of the Young Guard. In view of the new military operations that were to take place in Central Europe, Napoleon had to act very rapidly to reorganize his Imperial Guard. New regiments were formed from conscripts and with soldiers from the depots that had remained in France, who were added to the cadres of the old units and to the few veterans who had returned from Russia. At least 3,000 veterans of the line regiments who had been fighting against the British in Spain for many years were also transferred to the 'new' Imperial Guard. By January 1813, the Young Guard had been restructured on six regiments of Tirailleurs and six regiments of Voltigeurs; in addition, a new 7th Regiment of Tirailleurs was created by converting Pupilles and a new 7th Regiment of Voltigeurs was formed by converting National Guardsmen. Neither of these units had participated in the 1812 campaign. It almost seemed that Napoleon wanted to transform the entire French Army into his Imperial Guard, as during 1813 he continued to use all the new recruits to form new infantry corps for the Young Guard. He created the 8th Regiment of Tirailleurs and 8th Regiment of Voltigeurs in March 1813, plus a new unit of Flanqueurs. The latter received the official denomination of Regiment of Flanqueurs-Grenadiers, while the Flanqueur regiment that already existed was given a new name, the Regiment of Flanqueurs-Chasseurs. The former was attached to the Foot Grenadiers, the latter to the Foot Chasseurs. The new unit of Flanqueurs had two battalions with four companies each, later increased to six like in the existing Flanqueur regiment. During the second half of 1813, the emperor continued to expand the infantry of the Young Guard, creating five new regiments of Tirailleurs and five new regiments of Voltigeurs (both numbered 9–13). By now, however, these units were practically impossible to distinguish from those of the line infantry, except for their official denomination and peculiar uniforms. Only the Old Guard and Middle Guard retained a true elite status like before the 1812 campaign. After the great expansion of 1813, the Imperial Guard alone represented one-third of the French Army. During the campaign of 1814, which was fought on French soil, the inexperienced conscripts of the Young Guard fought with enormous courage on several occasions, being admired even by the oldest *grognards*.

All the new units of Tirailleurs and Voltigeurs had a regimental staff incorporating the following elements: one colonel, two chefs de bataillon, one major, one paymaster, one adjutant-major, one surgeon-major, one surgeon-assistant, four adjutants, one drum-corporal and one armourer. Each regiment comprised two battalions with four companies each. A single company included the following elements: one captain, two sub-lieutenants, one sergeant-major, four sergeants, one quartermaster, eight corporals, three drummers and 163 privates. From 1813–14, the Imperial Guard also featured a small foreign infantry unit known as the Polish Battalion, made up of Polish veteran soldiers who had fought under Napoleon during the Russian campaign and whose original corps had been destroyed during the retreat. Poland had ceased to exist as an independent kingdom in 1795, when it was partitioned for the third time between three of the major powers of Europe: Austria, Prussia and Russia. Since 1795, thousands of Polish exiles and volunteers had joined the ranks of the French Army, hoping that Revolutionary France could help them in their struggle to regain the independence of their homeland. After all, the enemies of Poland were also the enemies of the French Revolution. Napoleon had Polish military units under his command from 1796 and soon developed a great personal admiration for his Polish soldiers, who were extremely loyal and courageous. In 1807, after defeating the Russians at the Battle of Friedland, the emperor was finally able to recreate an independent Polish state in the heart of Europe: the Grand-Duchy of Warsaw. This was one of Napoleon's staunchest allies during the following years, forming an effective army that followed the emperor during his invasion of Russian. After the defeat of 1812, the Grand-Duchy of Warsaw was conquered by the Russians, and thereafter what remained of its military forces was absorbed into the French Army. These veterans, together with the survivors of a Polish corps that was part of the French Army – the so-called 'Vistula Legion' – were brought together to form the Polish Battalion of the Imperial Guard. This had an establishment of four companies and was attached to the 2nd Regiment of Foot Grenadiers, where it had the same pay and privileges. The Polish Battalion fought with enormous courage at the Battle of Leipzig in 1813 and was disbanded soon after due to the high rate of casualties it suffered.

During the French campaign of 1814, Napoleon, who was extremely happy with the

Sergeant-major of the Tirailleurs-Grenadiers.

The Infantry of the Middle Guard and Young Guard 49

Soldier of the Voltigeurs (left) and of the Tirailleurs-Grenadiers (right).

performance of the Young Guard, decided to expand it by creating the following new units: the 14th, 15th and 16th Regiment of Tirailleurs, and the 14th, 15th and 16th Regiment of Voltigeurs. Most of the new corps, however, never had enough soldiers and lacked most of the necessary officers; in addition, few of their members received proper training. The general situation of the French Army was desperate in 1814, but the emperor continued to create units of conscripts and to give them grand-sounding Guard denominations. Several members of the six new regiments created during 1814 came from the Spanish Royal Guard of Joseph Bonaparte, which had ceased to exist following Wellington's victories in the Iberian Peninsula. After invading the country in 1808, Napoleon had made his brother Joseph king of Spain and had given him veteran soldiers in order to create a Royal Guard. When this was disbanded, some of these battle-hardened veterans returned to France and were absorbed into the Young Guard.

With the first abdication of Napoleon, the entire Imperial Guard was disbanded and only 1,000 veterans continued to serve their emperor, being assembled into the Elba Battalion. This comprised the following sub-units: three companies of Foot Grenadiers, three companies of Foot Chasseurs, one squadron of lancers and one company of artillery. Unlike the regiments of the Old Guard, which were retained in service by the restored monarchy as part of the Royal Guard, those of the Middle Guard and Young Guard were not re-formed. In 1815, Napoleon returned to France and hastily reorganized his Imperial Guard; as we have seen in the previous chapter, he greatly enlarged the Foot Grenadiers and Foot Chasseurs, but also re-formed the regiments of Tirailleurs and Voltigeurs. Six regiments of Tirailleurs and six of Voltigeurs were organized, later both increased to eight for a total of sixteen foot units in the Young Guard. The emperor, however, had very little time to structure and train these new corps effectively. Consequently, only two regiments of Tirailleurs and two of Voltigeurs (all of which were understrength) could be deployed at the Battle of Waterloo. Despite this, the units of the Young Guard fought with great valour during the final clash of the 1815 campaign as they tried in vain to repulse the Prussian attack that decided the outcome of the battle.

Uniforms and equipment

The two infantry regiments of the Middle Guard, the Fusiliers-Grenadiers and the Fusiliers-Chasseurs, were dressed quite similarly to the Foot Grenadiers and Foot Chasseurs of the Old Guard, but wore the shako as headgear instead of the bearskin. The uniform of the Fusiliers-Grenadiers comprised the following: black shako with white cords, red plume, national cockade and brass frontal plate representing an Imperial eagle; dark blue tunic with dark blue collar and red round cuffs, red epaulettes with white crescent and fringes, white cuff flaps and white frontal lapels; white waistcoat; white trousers; black leggings; black shoes; and white leather belt equipment. The Fusiliers-Chasseurs were dressed as follows: black shako with white cords, red-and-green plume, national cockade and brass frontal plate representing an Imperial eagle; dark blue tunic with dark blue collar and red pointed cuffs (piped in white), green epaulettes with red crescent and fringes, and white frontal lapels; white waistcoat; white trousers; black leggings; black shoes; and white leather belt equipment.

The new units of Tirailleurs and Conscripts formed in 1809 were all dressed in entirely dark blue uniforms, like the light infantry regiments of the French Army, making them easily distinguishable from the foot units of the Old Guard and Middle Guard. The uniform of the Tirailleurs-Grenadiers comprised: black shako with white cords, white-and-red plume, national cockade and brass frontal plate representing an Imperial eagle; dark blue tunic with red collar piped in blue, red pointed cuffs piped in white, red shoulder straps piped in white and dark blue frontal lapels piped in white; white waistcoat; white trousers; black leggings; black shoes; and white leather belt equipment. The Tirailleurs-Chasseurs were dressed in a similar way: black shako with white cords, green plume, national cockade and brass frontal plate representing an Imperial eagle; dark blue tunic with red collar piped in blue, red pointed cuffs piped in white, green shoulder straps piped in white and dark blue frontal lapels piped in white; white waistcoat; white trousers; black leggings; black shoes; and white leather belt equipment. The Conscripts-Grenadiers were uniformed similarly to the Tirailleurs-Grenadiers: black shako with red cords, red pompom, national cockade and brass frontal plate representing an Imperial eagle; dark blue tunic with dark blue collar and dark blue frontal lapels without piping, red round cuffs and white cuff flaps, and dark blue shoulder straps piped in red; white waistcoat; white trousers; black short leggings with red lace and tassel; black shoes; and white leather belt equipment. The Conscripts-Chasseurs were dressed similarly to the Tirailleurs-Chasseurs: black shako with green cords, green pompom, national cockade and brass frontal plate representing an Imperial eagle; dark blue tunic with dark blue collar and dark blue frontal lapels without piping, red pointed cuffs with white piping and dark blue shoulder straps piped in green; dark blue waistcoat; dark blue trousers; black short leggings with green lace and tassel; black shoes; and white leather belt equipment.

The Velites of Turin and the Velites of Florence wore the same uniform: black shako with white cords, red plume, national cockade and brass frontal plate representing an Imperial eagle; dark blue tunic with dark blue collar and red round

Soldier of the Voltigeurs.

cuffs, red epaulettes, white cuff flaps and white frontal lapels; white waistcoat; white trousers; black leggings; black shoes; and white leather belt equipment. The National Guardsmen of the Imperial Guard were dressed as follows: black shako with white cords, pompom in company colour, national cockade and brass frontal plate representing an Imperial eagle; dark blue tunic with red collar and pointed cuffs both piped in white, dark blue shoulder straps piped in red and white frontal lapels piped in red; white waistcoat and trousers; black leggings; black shoes; and white leather belt equipment. The two battalions of this unit had the same internal organization as the line infantry battalions, which comprised one company of grenadiers and one of voltigeurs, in addition to four companies of fusiliers. Grenadiers wore the following peculiar elements: red pompom and cords of the shako, and red epaulettes instead of the shoulder straps. Voltigeurs had the following peculiar elements: light green pompom and cords of the shako, and light green epaulettes instead of the shoulder straps.

The new regiments of Tirailleurs and Voltigeurs organized after 1810 were all dressed in light infantry style. The Tirailleurs wore the following: black shako with red pompom, national cockade and brass frontal plate representing an Imperial eagle; dark blue tunic with red collar piped in blue, red pointed cuffs piped in white, red shoulder straps piped in white and dark blue frontal lapels piped in white; white waistcoat; white trousers; black leggings; black shoes; and white leather belt equipment. The Voltigeurs were uniformed as follows: black shako with red-and-green plume, national cockade and brass frontal plate representing an Imperial eagle; dark blue tunic with yellow collar piped in green, red pointed cuffs piped in white, green epaulettes with yellow crescent and dark blue frontal lapels piped in white; white waistcoat; white trousers; black leggings; black shoes; and white leather belt equipment. All the regiments of Tirailleurs and Voltigeurs received new tunics in 1813, with the frontal lapels united into a single plastron; these had been given to the regiments of line infantry since 1812, according to the dress regulations that were promulgated during that year.

The Pupilles of the Imperial Guard wore two different uniforms: a dark green one that was used by the battalions numbered 1–4 and a white one by the battalions numbered 5–8. The depot battalion of this corps had various companies dressed in the dark green uniform and others in the white one. The green uniform was as follows: black shako with green pompom and cords, national cockade and brass frontal plate representing an Imperial eagle; dark green tunic with yellow piping to collar, pointed cuffs, shoulders straps and frontal lapels (the latter united into a single plastron); white trousers; black short leggings; black shoes; and white leather belt equipment. The white uniform consisted of the following: black shako with green pompom,

Soldier of the Conscripts-Chasseurs (left) and of the Flanqueurs-Chasseurs (right).

white cords, national cockade and brass frontal plate representing an Imperial eagle; white tunic with dark green collar, round cuffs and frontal lapels (the latter united into a single plastron), and white shoulder straps piped in dark green; white trousers; black short leggings; black shoes; and white leather belt equipment. Members of the Bataillon d'Instruction retained the uniforms of their original regiments and thus had no distinctive dress.

The Flanqueurs-Chasseurs were dressed in dark green, with uniforms in perfect light-infantry style: black shako with green-and-yellow pompom, green cords, national cockade and brass frontal plate representing an Imperial eagle; dark green tunic with yellow piping to collar, pointed cuffs, shoulders straps and frontal lapels (the latter united into a single plastron); white trousers; black short leggings with yellow lacing and tassel; black shoes; and white leather belt equipment. The Flanqueurs-Grenadiers were uniformed in a similar way: black shako with red-and-yellow pompom, red cords, national cockade and brass frontal plate representing an Imperial eagle; dark green tunic with yellow piping to collar, pointed cuffs, shoulders straps and frontal lapels (the latter united into a single plastron); white trousers; black short leggings with yellow lacing and tassel; black shoes; and white leather belt equipment. The soldiers of the Polish Battalion of the Imperial Guard retained the uniforms of their previous units, which were the infantry regiments of the Grand-Duchy of Warsaw and the Vistula Legion.

Chapter 4

The Mounted Grenadiers

History and organization

Grenadiers emerged as a new troop type of the infantry during the second half of the seventeenth century, when various European armies started to employ hand-grenades as a weapon. These could be thrown by infantrymen and were quite simple to produce. They could be of great use during siege operations and could also be used during pitched battles to destroy field fortifications. In order to use the new grenades more effectively, the infantry units of the European armies started to select the tallest and strongest men among their members; these were retrained as grenadiers and learned how to use hand-grenades on the battlefield. This development took place during the second half of the seventeenth century, when the dominant military power of Europe was the Kingdom of France, ruled by the 'Sun King', Louis XIV, who had the most innovative military force of the age. It was the first to introduce military uniforms in the modern sense of the term (in 1660) and the first to create independent units of grenadiers inside the infantry regiments. From 1667, four men in each French infantry regiment started to be trained as grenadiers, and a company of grenadiers was included in each infantry battalion in 1671. During the following decades, grenadiers became the elite of the French foot troops thanks to their superior training and discipline. Over time, the French innovations were adopted by other European armies, and thus grenadiers could be found practically everywhere around the continent. Many monarchs later transformed their units of grenadiers into elite corps with 'guard' status and thus this new category of 'heavy infantry' became increasingly popular. Louis XIV was no exception to this rule, since in 1676 he created a company of 250 horse grenadiers inside his large Royal Household. The new corps was formed by assembling the best foot grenadiers from all the battalions of the French line infantry. Originally, the Horse Grenadiers of the Royal Guard were trained to act as a sort of mounted infantry: they moved on horses but fought on foot like ordinary grenadiers. However, they were gradually transformed into a heavy cavalry force tasked with charging the enemy in close formation, and the use of hand-grenades declined in importance. Meanwhile, the popularity of the foot grenadiers rapidly increased in all the armies of Europe. They started to receive distinctive uniforms that comprised pointed mitre caps, which were designed to allow a grenadier to sling his musket on his back and throw grenades over-arm. During the eighteenth century, this kind of headgear was replaced by the new bearskin bonnet, which was designed to exaggerate the already impressive height of the soldiers who had been chosen to serve as grenadiers. The eighteenth century was a golden age for these elite soldiers, who became famous around the world for their combat capabilities. The grenadiers of Frederick the Great, in Prussia, were a model for those of all other armies. In France, from 1748, the infantry began to include an independent regiment known as the Grenadiers de France, entirely formed of grenadiers. By 1789, however, the use of hand-grenades had greatly declined across Europe, and thus the grenadiers had partly changed their nature: now they were elite infantry with superior training and impressive uniforms, but their tactical role was practically the same as the ordinary line infantry. At the outbreak of the French Revolution, the Horse Grenadiers of the Royal Guard had already been disbanded in order to cut economic costs, and thus the French Army no longer had any mounted grenadiers. This situation continued until October 1796, when the Guard of the Executive Directorate was created. This comprised a new unit of Mounted Grenadiers, made up of two companies and having a total of 120 men. The original denomination of the new corps was the Mounted Guard of the Directory, but this was soon changed to Mounted Grenadiers. When the Guard of the Executive Directorate was abolished by Napoleon in 1799, its Mounted Grenadiers consisted of the following elements: two captains, two lieutenants, two sub-lieutenants, two sergeant-majors, four sergeants, two quartermasters, eight corporals, four trumpeters and ninety troopers.

At the time of the creation of the new Consular Guard, the Mounted Grenadiers consisted of two squadrons and comprised the following members: one colonel, two squadron-leaders, one adjutant-major, two standard-bearers, one adjutant and one trumpet-corporal. Each of the two squadrons had two companies and each of these included one captain, one first-lieutenant, one second-lieutenant, one sub-lieutenant, one sergeant-major, four sergeants, one quartermaster, eight corporals, one farrier, two trumpeters, one barber and sixty-four troopers. In January 1800, the number of troopers in each company was increased from to ninety-six. Some months later, in April, the Mounted Grenadiers received their baptism of fire during Napoleon's second Italian campaign. This culminated in the French victory at the Battle of Marengo, during which the Mounted Grenadiers launched a deadly counter-charge against the Austrian cavalry and won the personal admiration of the First Consul. In September 1800, after returning to France, Napoleon expanded his Consular Guard, and the Mounted Grenadiers were also affected by this process. The establishment of the unit was increased to three squadrons with two companies each. A single

Soldier of the Mounted Grenadiers.

company included the following elements: one captain, one first-lieutenant, one second-lieutenant, one sub-lieutenant, one sergeant-major, four sergeants, one quartermaster, eight corporals, two trumpeters, one farrier and ninety-six troopers. In November 1801, the Mounted Grenadiers of the Consular Guard were reorganized in order to become a regiment, together with the Mounted Chasseurs; as a result, by March of the following year, they had a new and larger establishment, with four squadrons of two companies each. In May 1802, the number of officers and NCOs in each company was slightly increased, but the general structure of the regiment was unchanged. Shortly before the Consular Guard was transformed into the Imperial Guard, the Mounted Grenadiers had a regimental staff with the following elements: one colonel, four squadron-leaders, one quartermaster, one captain-instructor, one major, one adjutant-major, one lieutenant, one sub-lieutenant, two standard-bearers, one first-class surgeon, one second-class surgeon, one sergeant-instructor, one sergeant-quartermaster, one veterinary, one assistant-veterinary, one trumpet-major, two trumpet-corporals, three mounted craftsmen and four unmounted craftsmen. In total, the whole unit had 1,015 officers, NCOs and soldiers.

The Mounted Grenadiers were probably the most impressive military unit of the newly established Imperial Guard, at least from an aesthetic point of view: they were mounted on big black horses from the countryside of Normandy and wore tall bearskins, together with long black leather boots that covered the knee. While moving across the streets of Paris, they gave a very vivid picture of what heavy cavalry was. The horses of the Mounted Grenadiers were probably the best of the whole French Army; they had full manes and tails, which were adorned with red ribbons and rosettes during parades. The soldiers of the regiment had several nicknames, including 'the Giants' and 'the Gods', but the most popular one was 'les Gros Talons', or 'the High Heels', that derived from the size of their boots. It was extremely difficult to become a member of the Mounted Grenadiers, due to the strict requirements to enter the ranks of this elite corps: a candidate had to be at least 1.76 metres tall, have ten years' service in the army, combat experience in four campaigns and at least one official citation for bravery. On 19 September 1805, Napoleon decided to expand the cavalry of his Imperial Guard by creating a new Corps of Mounted Velites, which was quite short-lived. This, like its infantry equivalent, was made up of young volunteers from the richest families of France. In order to be admitted into the ranks of the Mounted Velites and start a promising military career, they had to pay a sum of money. The new corps consisted of 800 men, organized into two squadrons with four companies each (later reduced to two); the first squadron was attached to the Regiment of Mounted Grenadiers, the second to the Regiment of Mounted Chasseurs. In 1805, the Mounted Grenadiers fought at the Battle of Austerlitz, during which they charged with two squadrons against the cavalry of the Russian Imperial Guard, proving their courage and obtaining a clear victory over their direct opponents.

In 1807, the Regiment of Mounted Grenadiers played a decisive part in the Battle of Eylau, at which Napoleon came very near to defeat. At a critical point of the clash, trying to stabilize the situation along his front, the emperor ordered a massive charge of his cavalry reserves, under the command of Marshal Murat. After breaking

Soldier of the Mounted Grenadiers in parade dress.

the enemy lines during a snowstorm, the Mounted Grenadiers were surrounded by cavalry units of the Russian reserve but refused to surrender and instead counter-charged. Thanks to their bravery, they were able to escape capture and helped give their emperor enough time to defeat the Russians. After the great victories of 1805–07, Napoleon ordered each of his regiments of cuirassiers and carabiniers to send ten of their best men for service in the Mounted Grenadiers, thereby replenishing the casualties suffered by the unit during the previous campaigns. The Mounted Grenadiers participated in operations in Spain and Central Europe in 1809, but did not fight at the Battle of Wagram. They then returned for a short period to Spain before being recalled to France. From 1 July 1811, no further volunteers were admitted into the ranks of the Corps of Mounted Velites; those who were already part of this corps were gradually absorbed into the Guard or line cavalry regiments after receiving commissions as officers. On 1 January 1812, all remaining Velites who were still attached to the Regiment of Mounted Grenadiers were brought together to form a new 5th squadron of the Grenadiers. During the 1812 campaign in Russia, the Mounted Grenadiers did not take part in any of the major battles, but did fight on several occasions during the long retreat that followed the occupation of Moscow. By the end of the campaign, the regiment had been greatly reduced in numbers.

Napoleon worked hard to reorganize the Mounted Grenadiers as soon as possible by searching for cavalry veterans in every corner of his crumbling empire. Each of the thirty French cavalry regiments that were serving against Wellington in the Iberian Peninsula were required to send five of their best men to France, in order to augment the effective strength of the Imperial Guard's cavalry. Thanks to this and other similar measures, the emperor was able to rebuild his Regiment of Mounted Grenadiers on five squadrons; he was even able to create a new 6th squadron with 300 young recruits, who were called 'Second Grenadiers' by their senior comrades and received the same pay as standard cavalrymen of the line. Formally, only the officers and NCOs of this new squadron were members of the Old Guard, the rest of their regiment – the young recruits – being formally part of the Young Guard. During the 1813 German campaign and that of 1814 in France, the Mounted Grenadiers fought extremely well on several occasions, suffering heavy casualties. Napoleon continued to substitute the fallen soldiers of the unit with veterans coming from Spain or with young recruits, but the general quality of his forces was rapidly declining. With the restoration of the Bourbon monarchy that put Louis XVIII on the French throne, the Regiment of Mounted Grenadiers was transformed into the Corps of Royal Cuirassiers, which consisted of four squadrons with two companies each. Most of the unit's veterans resented the rule of the new monarchy, partly because their pay was reduced significantly. The distinctive uniform that had been worn until then by the

Mounted Grenadiers was replaced by a new one, but the massive bearskin was retained after troopers from the regiment protested against the adoption of new headgear. When Napoleon returned to France in 1815, the former Mounted Grenadiers were among the first to support him. The squadron of Second Grenadiers, which had been disbanded by Louis XVIII, was reorganized by the Emperor and the regiment participated in the Battle of Waterloo with five squadrons. Like other units of the Imperial Guard cavalry, the Mounted Grenadiers charged several times against the defensive squares of the British infantry but without forcing a breakthrough. After Napoleon's second abdication, the unit was disbanded along with the rest of the Imperial Guard during the closing months of 1815.

Uniforms and equipment

The uniform of the Mounted Grenadiers remained practically the same during the whole Napoleonic period, and always comprised a black bearskin as headgear. The Mounted Grenadiers of the Guard of the Executive Directorate were dressed as follows: black bearskin with orange cords, national cockade and red plume; dark blue tunic with red collar piped in white, red round cuffs, white cuff flaps, white frontal lapels (piped in red), orange *contré-epaulettes* and orange *aiguillettes* (decorative cords) worn on the right shoulder; white waistcoat; white trousers; black leather tall boots; and white leather belt equipment. The shabraque worn under the saddle was dark blue with orange external edging. The new uniform adopted by the Mounted Grenadiers of the Consular Guard, which remained the same after the creation of the Imperial Guard, was not so different from that described above: black bearskin with orange cords, national cockade and red plume; dark blue tunic with dark blue collar, red round cuffs, white cuff flaps, white frontal lapels (without piping), orange *contre-épaulettes* and orange *aiguillettes* worn on the right shoulder; white waistcoat; buff trousers; black leather tall boots; and white leather belt equipment. The shabraque was dark blue with orange external edging, having an orange flaming grenade in the rear corner. On campaign, the dark blue tunic was replaced by a single-breasted *surtout* in the same colour, which had collar and round cuffs without piping. *Contre-épaulettes* and *aiguillettes* were also worn on the *surtout*; the latter, in particular, a mark of distinction of the Old Guard's cavalry which was not found on the uniforms of the Second Grenadiers (who as we have seen belonged to the Young Guard from an administrative point of view). When on campaign, the red plume of the bearskin was removed and the buff trousers were replaced by grey overalls. In winter, all ranks wore the greatcoat, which was light grey with orange frontal frogging for the Mounted Grenadiers. Like all other units of the French Army, they also had the

Trumpeter of the Mounted Grenadiers.

fatigue cap known as the *bonnet de police*, which was dark blue with orange piping and frontal tassel, bearing on the front a flaming grenade embroidered in orange. The trumpeters of the Mounted Grenadiers wore a very peculiar uniform, which was quite different from that of the ordinary troopers. It consisted of a black bicorn with national cockade, golden edging and white plume; medium blue tunic with red collar and round cuffs piped in gold, red frontal lapels with golden piping to external edges and buttonholes, red-and-golden *contre-épaulettes* and red-and-golden *aiguillettes*; white waistcoat; buff trousers; black leather boots; and white belt equipment. The shabraque was red with golden external edging. On campaign, the trumpeters wore a *surtout*, which was medium blue in their case, while their overalls, worn instead of the trousers, were medium blue and not grey. The bicorn was only used by trumpeters on parade; while on campaign, the standard black bearskin was worn. All Mounted Grenadiers always wore white gloves, which were a distinctive element of their dress.

Chapter 5

The Mounted Chasseurs

History and organization

The Mounted Chasseurs were undoubtedly Napoleon's favourite unit of the Imperial Guard. The veteran soldiers of this corps had followed him since 1796, when he was just a young and inexperienced general. Originally raised as the Guides of Bonaparte, the Mounted Chasseurs protected Napoleon as his mounted bodyguard until the Battle of Waterloo in 1815. They saved him from certain death on several occasions, and always served with great professionalism. The cavalry troop type known as 'mounted chasseurs' appeared for the first time in the French Army in 1743, when an early independent corps of horse skirmishers was created. In subsequent years, particularly during the course of the Seven Years' War (1756–63), the major European armies started to understand the tactical importance of light units (both on foot and mounted). They learned from combat experience that lightly armed soldiers – possibly equipped with rifled weapons – could perform special duties that were inappropriate for line infantry or heavy cavalry. Scouting and skirmishing, two tactical functions that have been fundamental for all armies through history, needed specifically trained corps. As a result, the first light infantry and light cavalry units started to appear in the major European armies. In 1776, several of the new light cavalry corps of the French Army were drawn together in order to form twenty-four squadrons of Mounted Chasseurs. This measure was introduced to create a more stable light cavalry force, since the previous independent units had always been small and temporary corps whose reliability was not impressive. The new squadrons of Mounted Chasseurs were not designed to act as independent corps, since each of them was attached to a regiment of dragoons. At the time, they were still considered as an auxiliary component of the line cavalry and thus were organized in small units. Soon, however, the Mounted Chasseurs showed their great combat capabilities and tactical flexibility; consequently, in 1779, their twenty-four squadrons were detached from the units of dragoons and combined in order to form six independent regiments of Mounted Chasseurs. In 1788, shortly before the outbreak of the French Revolution, six regiments of dragoons were transformed into units of Mounted Chasseurs. They thus had a total of twelve regiments when the French Revolution began in 1789.

During the Revolutionary Wars, the Mounted Chasseurs were expanded to twenty-five regiments and became increasingly popular, particularly because of their great flexibility: they could fight on foot as light infantrymen, act as mounted scouts and also charge the enemy if required by circumstances.

As we have seen, the Mounted Chasseurs of the Imperial Guard had a very long history, which commenced during the first Italian campaign of 1796–97. The young General Bonaparte, after assuming command of the Army of Italy, organized his own Corps of Guides. Since April 1792, the officers commanding French armies on the field had been permitted by the central government to create their own independent units of guides, recruited from volunteers, who acted both as explorers and bodyguards for the general staff of each commander. Napoleon was no exception to this rule and soon created a Corps of Guides for himself that would later assume the denomination of Guides of Bonaparte. Initially, for personal protection, Napoleon had just two companies of picked foot grenadiers and fifty Guides on horse. Later, on 25 September 1796, the mounted members of the Guides of Bonaparte were for the first time formally organized as a squadron, comprising the following elements: one squadron-leader, one captain, one lieutenant, two sub-lieutenants, one sergeant-major, six sergeants, eight corporals, one veterinary, two farriers, one saddler, two harness-makers and 136 troopers. The troopers were chosen from the best elements of the French line cavalry regiments serving in the Army of Italy. During the military operations of 1797, the Guides of Bonaparte distinguished themselves on several occasions, Napoleon frequently employing them to perform special missions.

The Guides of Bonaparte also followed their general during the Egyptian campaign that began in 1798, during which their mounted component was increased to five companies, each of which included the following: one captain, one lieutenant, two sub-lieutenants and 112 NCOs/troopers/trumpeters. Like during the earlier Italian campaign, members of the Guides were chosen from the best elements of the line cavalry regiments serving under Napoleon. The Guides of Bonaparte fought with distinction in Egypt, despite the extreme temperatures and the inhospitable nature of the desert. When Napoleon left the country, most of his Guides remained in North Africa, where they continued to fight until the final surrender of the French forces in Egypt. Some picked elements of the corps, however, followed Napoleon to France: 112 mounted and 120 foot Guides were chosen for their long service and great loyalty towards Bonaparte. After creating the Consulate with a military coup, Napoleon organized the new Consular Guard by assembling together the Guard of the Executive Directorate and the Guard of the Legislative Corps. However, they lacked light units, which was a serious deficiency, so the new First Consul decided to use his veteran Guides to form two light infantry corps inside the Consular Guard.

The Mounted Chasseurs 67

Soldier of the Mounted Chasseurs.

The mounted Guides received the new denomination of Mounted Chasseurs and were initially organized in a single company, with four officers and 113 troopers. A few months later, at the Battle of Marengo, the young Consular Guard was tested on the field and the Mounted Chasseurs performed extremely well. After this early success, they were expanded and became a squadron with two companies, each having one captain, three lieutenants and 117 NCOs/troopers/trumpeters. In August 1801, a second squadron was added to the Mounted Chasseurs and was given the following staff: one squadron-leader, one adjutant-major, two sub-lieutenants, two standard-bearers, one trumpet-corporal, one master tailor, one master bootmaker, one master saddler and one master armourer. A single company comprised one captain, one first-lieutenant, one second-lieutenant, one sub-lieutenant, one sergeant-major, four sergeants, one quartermaster, eight corporals, one farrier, two trumpeters and ninety-six troopers. In November 1801, the Mounted Chasseurs received regimental status but continued to be made up of just two squadrons. This changed in October 1802, when the number of squadrons was increased to four.

After the transformation of the Consular Guard into the Imperial Guard, the Mounted Chasseurs retained their previous internal establishment with very few modifications. On 19 September 1805, Napoleon ordered the creation of two Velite companies within the Mounted Chasseurs; these, like the other two serving with the Mounted Grenadiers, were made up of volunteer gentlemen who wished to initiate a military career in the French Army. The two companies serving with each regiment were joined together to form a squadron, but did not operate as an independent unit since its members were distributed among the veteran squadrons. Each company of the squadron could thus achieve a larger establishment with 125 men in time of war. The Mounted Chasseurs did not happily accept the presence of the Velites, considering these young volunteers to be inept gentlemen who knew very little of real life. However, the Velites eventually became a stable component of the regiment. During the 1805 campaign, the Regiment of Mounted Chasseurs fought extremely well, especially during the Battle of Austerlitz when it counter-charged the cavalry of the Russian Imperial Guard together with the Mamelukes and Mounted Grenadiers. This impressive action was admired by all the soldiers of the Grande Armée, but also by their opponents, who could not fail to recognize the valour of Napoleon's Imperial Guard. The Mounted Chasseurs had reached the pinnacle of fame within the French cavalry and were ready to fight again for the glory of their emperor. Napoleon had a very special personal relationship with his mounted bodyguards, wearing their dark green uniform on most occasions and calling them by name. Ensuring the safety of Napoleon, by following him practically everywhere, was not a simple task: the Emperor was active twenty-four hours a day, every single day of the year, and during

The Mounted Chasseurs

Mounted Chasseur (left), Napoleon (centre) and Murat (right).

battles, he frequently exposed himself to enemy fire and did not show the same fear as other commanders.

At Eylau, in 1807, the Mounted Chasseurs took part in the epic charge of the French cavalry that was led by Murat and suffered heavy casualties. Their participation in the battle, like that of the Mounted Grenadiers, was fundamental in Napoleon avoiding defeat. In 1808, the Regiment of Mounted Chasseurs took part in the French invasion of Spain, during which it fought on several occasions, always with great distinction. The unit moved to Central Europe in 1809 in order to participate in the campaign against Austria, and fought at the decisive Battle of Wagram, where it charged Austrian infantry units deployed in square formation and suffered severe losses. Throughout 1810 and 1811, except for some small detachments that were sent to serve in Spain, the Mounted Chasseurs of the Imperial Guard remained in France to perform their regular escort duties. After 1 July 1811, no further volunteers were admitted into the ranks of the regiment's Velites. Those who were already part of the Velites were gradually absorbed into the Guard or line cavalry regiments after receiving commissions as officers. On 1 January 1812, all the remaining Velites who were still attached to the Regiment of Mounted Chasseurs were assembled together to form a new 5th squadron of the Chasseurs. During the 1812 campaign in Russia, Napoleon kept his Mounted Chasseurs in reserve and thus the regiment did not take part in the bloody Battle of Borodino. The second part of the campaign, with the slow retreat of the Grande Armée towards Poland, saw the Mounted Chasseurs escorting the Emperor in very difficult conditions. Russian Cossacks frequently attacked the retreating French columns, using hit-and-run tactics and organizing ambushes. Sometimes even Napoleon and his personal staff were menaced by these incursions, obliging the Mounted Chasseurs to act very rapidly in order to preserve the life of their beloved emperor. Unlike the other units of the Imperial Guard, however, the Regiment of Mounted Chasseurs did not suffer extremely high casualties in Russia.

Napoleon rebuilt his Imperial Guard in January 1813 by using all available resources; since the Mounted Chasseurs were still in a relatively good condition, the emperor decided to expand their usual establishment by creating three new squadrons. Another squadron was added in March of the same year, bringing the total to nine plus the single squadron of Mamelukes, which had always been attached to the Regiment of Mounted Chasseurs. Since each squadron had a total of 250 men, the expanded Mounted Chasseurs had an impressive establishment of some 2,500 soldiers and were the strongest mounted unit of the Imperial Guard. The first five squadrons, which were already in existence before 1812, were part of the Old Guard and continued to enjoy all the privileges of the latter's members; the squadrons numbered 6–9, however, were (at least from an administrative point of view) part of the Young Guard since their members were all young recruits. These younger squadrons were commonly

The Mounted Chasseurs 71

Soldier of the Mounted Chasseurs with second uniform.

known as the Second Mounted Chasseurs and received the same standard pay as the line cavalrymen. During the German campaign of 1813, the Mounted Chasseurs fought in the Battle of Leipzig, inflicting severe losses on the Russians and Swedes who tried to break the French lines in their sector. In 1814, with the first abdication of Napoleon, the Second Mounted Chasseurs were disbanded and the regiment was reduced to a peacetime establishment of just fifty-five officers and 644 rankers. In addition, the standard pay of the unit was greatly reduced and all the privileges enjoyed by its members were cancelled. When Napoleon returned to France after his first exile, the Mounted Chasseurs rejoined their emperor and were reorganized like the rest of the Imperial Guard. The four squadrons of Second Mounted Chasseurs, which had been broken up by Louis XVIII, were re-formed and assembled together in order to create a new and independent regiment. Consequently, during the 1815 campaign, the Imperial Guard comprised a 1st Regiment of Mounted Chasseurs in the Old Guard and a 2nd Regiment of Mounted Chasseurs in the Young Guard. The former unit took part in the Battle of Waterloo, joining the massive cavalry charges launched by Ney against Wellington's British infantry squares. While the French massed cavalry attacks were a great demonstration of courage, they actually achieved nothing: the British troops kept their positions and the battle was eventually lost for Napoleon. The Regiment of Mounted Chasseurs, like all the other units of the Old Guard, was disbanded in October and November 1815.

Uniforms and equipment

From their foundation, the Guides of Bonaparte had a dark green uniform with red facings in perfect 'mounted chasseur' style. This existed in two different versions, one for the foot Guides and another for the mounted Guides. The uniform of the foot Guides comprised the following elements: black bicorn with national cockade and red-and-green plume; dark green tunic with red collar and red pointed cuffs, dark green frontal lapels piped in red and red *contre-épaulettes*; red waistcoat with decorative frogging on the front in the same colour; red trousers with decorative 'Hungarian' knots embroidered on the front; black leather short boots with red edging and frontal tassel; and white leather belt equipment. The uniform of the mounted Guides was slightly different: black bicorn with national cockade and red-and-green plume; dark green tunic with red collar and red pointed cuffs, dark green frontal lapels piped in red, red *contre-epaulettes* and red *aiguillettes* worn on the right shoulder; red waistcoat with decorative frogging on the front in the same colour; dark green trousers with red piping and decorative 'Hungarian' knots embroidered on the front; black leather short boots with red edging and frontal tassel; and white leather belt equipment. The shabraque was dark green with red external edging. On campaign, the decorated waistcoat was replaced by a simpler version, which was double-breasted and had no frontal frogging, while the standard trousers were not used, being replaced by dark green overalls that had a reinforcement of black leather in the internal part. During the Egyptian campaign, most of the mounted Guides added a white cloak, produced locally, to their usual outfit. The drummers of the foot Guides had the following uniform: black bicorn edged in gold with national cockade and light blue-and-red plume; light blue tunic with red collar and red pointed cuffs piped in gold, light blue frontal lapels piped in red and golden *contre-épaulettes*; red waistcoat with decorative frogging on the front in gold; red trousers with golden decorative 'Hungarian' knots embroidered on the front; black leather short boots with golden edging and frontal tassel; and white leather belt equipment. The trumpeters of the mounted Guides were dressed quite similarly to the drummers: black bicorn edged in gold with national cockade and light blue-and-red plume; light blue tunic with red collar and red pointed cuffs piped in gold, light blue frontal lapels piped in red, golden *contre-épaulettes* and golden *aiguillettes* on the right shoulder; red waistcoat with decorative frogging on the front in gold, light blue trousers with golden decorative 'Hungarian' knots embroidered on the front; black leather short boots with golden edging and frontal tassel; and white leather belt equipment.

The Mounted Chasseurs of the newly raised Consular Guard received a new uniform in perfect hussar-style, which was retained with very little modification until the end of the Napoleonic era in 1815. This was extremely elegant and comprised two main elements, the dolman and the pelisse, both derived from the traditional dress of the Magyar hussars, the light cavalrymen who first appeared in Hungary during the fifteenth century. The dolman was a jacket cut tight and short, decorated with multiple rows of buttons (usually three) and with stripes of frogging on the front. The pelisse was a short fur-trimmed jacket that was worn hanging loose over the left shoulder. The headgear of the new uniform was a busby covered with black fur. The Mounted Chasseurs were particularly proud of their dress, which retained the same colours worn by the Guides of Bonaparte (dark green and red): black busby with red-and-green plume, orange cords and red soft 'bag' having piping and decorative tassel in orange; dark green dolman with dark green collar and red pointed cuffs all piped in orange, and orange frontal frogging connecting five vertical rows of buttons; red pelisse trimmed with black fur and having orange piping to the seams, plus orange frontal frogging connecting two vertical rows of buttons; red trousers with orange piping and decorative 'Hungarian' knots embroidered on the front; orange-and-green sash worn wrapped around the waist; black leather short boots with orange edging and frontal tassel; and white leather belt equipment. The shabraque was dark green with orange external edging, having an orange bugle horn embroidered on the back corner. The standard equipment of the Mounted Chasseurs also included a small bag, known as a sabretache, which was used to transport documents. Originally this was red, with orange external edging and the coat-of-arms of the French Republic

Trumpeter of the Mounted Chasseurs.

embroidered on the front; with the proclamation of the Empire, it became dark green with orange external edging and the Imperial coat-of-arms embroidered on the front.

The Mounted Chasseurs of the Imperial Guard had a uniform that was quite similar to that worn previously: black busby with red-and-green plume, orange cords and red soft 'bag' having piping and decorative tassel in orange; dark green dolman with dark green collar and red pointed cuffs all piped in orange, plus orange frontal frogging connecting five vertical rows of buttons; red pelisse trimmed with black fur and having orange piping to the seams, and orange frontal frogging connecting two vertical rows of buttons; buff trousers; orange-and-green sash worn wrapped around the waist; black leather short boots with orange edging and frontal tassel; and white leather belt equipment. The shabraque was dark green with orange external edging, having an orange Imperial Eagle embroidered on the back corner. The Mounted Chasseurs of the Imperial Guard, in addition to their usual hussar-style dress, also had a more simple uniform that was worn on campaign and was quite similar to the original dress of the Guides of Bonaparte. This comprised the following elements: black busby with red-and-green plume, orange cords and red soft 'bag' having piping and decorative tassel in orange; dark green tunic with red collar and pointed cuffs, dark green frontal lapels piped in red, plus orange *aiguillettes* worn on the left shoulder; red waistcoat with orange piping and frontal frogging; dark green trousers with orange piping and decorative 'Hungarian' knots embroidered on the front; black leather short boots with orange edging and frontal tassel; and white leather belt equipment. Napoleon regularly wore this uniform, albeit with some personal variations: instead of the busby he used a black bicorn with national cockade, while his waistcoat and trousers were entirely white. On campaign, the decorated waistcoat was replaced by a simpler version which was double-breasted and had no frontal frogging, and the standard trousers were not used, being replaced by dark green overalls that had an internal reinforcement of black leather. The officers of the Mounted Chasseurs wore the same uniforms as their men, but all the orange elements of the dress were golden for them. The Second Mounted Chasseurs were dressed like the veterans of the 1st Regiment, but had a red cylindrical shako as distinctive headgear.

The trumpeters of the Regiment of Mounted Chasseurs wore one of the most elegant uniforms of the whole French Army. This was in hussar-style and consisted of the following elements: white busby with light blue-and-red plume, golden cords and red soft 'bag' having piping and decorative tassel in gold; light blue dolman with red collar and red pointed cuffs all piped in gold, and golden frontal frogging connecting five vertical rows of buttons; red pelisse trimmed with white fur and having golden piping to the seams, plus golden frontal frogging connecting two vertical rows of buttons; buff trousers; gold-and-light blue sash worn wrapped around the waist; black leather short boots with golden edging and frontal tassel; and white leather belt equipment. The shabraque was red with golden external edging, having a golden Imperial Eagle embroidered on the back corner. The sabretache was red with golden external edging and the Imperial coat-of-arms embroidered on the front. The trumpeters had a simpler second uniform that was mostly worn on campaign: black busby with light blue-and-red plume, golden cords and red soft 'bag' having piping and decorative tassel in gold; light blue tunic with red collar and pointed cuffs piped in gold, light blue frontal lapels piped in gold, golden *contre-épaulettes* plus golden *aiguillettes* worn on the left shoulder; red waistcoat with golden piping and frontal frogging; light blue trousers with golden piping and decorative 'Hungarian' knots embroidered on the front; black leather short boots with golden edging and frontal tassel; and white leather belt equipment.

Chapter 6

The Empress' Dragoons

History and organization

The first units of dragoons appeared in European armies during the closing phase of the Thirty Years' War, the bloody conflict that ravaged most of Germany between 1618 and 1648. The basic idea behind the formation of the first dragoon corps was that of having some soldiers who could move on horses but fight on foot. The armies of the time increasingly needed highly mobile troops who could travel long distances in a short time but could also fight as standard infantry when needed. As a result, the first companies of dragoons were created: these consisted of ordinary infantrymen who knew how to ride a horse and could perform as mounted infantry. The term 'dragoons' derived from the multi-tasking nature of these new soldiers: like the mythical beasts giving them their name, which were capable of living on earth as well as on water, the dragoons could be employed as infantry but also as cavalry. One of the first armies to include these new soldiers on a large scale was the French one of Louis XIV, which already had two independent regiments of dragoons by 1660. Initially, these new corps had much more in common with the infantry than with the cavalry: they did not wear boots like ordinary mounted troops, they were organized in companies and not in squadrons, their musicians were drummers and not trumpeters, and their main weapon was an infantry musket rather than a cavalry sword. During the eighteenth century, the dragoons changed their nature as they started to be employed as mounted infantrymen only very rarely. On most occasions they were asked to act as regular cavalry, being tasked with frontal charges and other tactical functions that were typical of mounted 'shock' troops. The dragoons gradually became a sort of 'medium' cavalry: they had lighter equipment than the heavy cavalry cuirassiers but heavier equipment than the light cavalry hussars. As a result, a dragoon unit could attack the enemy with a charge but could also conduct some skirmishing operations. Only in France did the dragoons always retain part of their original mounted infantry function, unlike in other European countries. In the French Army, dragoons were equipped with bayonets and could fight dismounted if needed. Napoleon continued this French tradition, and during his period as Emperor he frequently employed

Soldier of the Empress' Dragoons with parade dress.

his dragoons as normal infantrymen. Before the outbreak of revolution in 1789, the French dragoons wore a distinctive dark green uniform that would be retained with minor modifications until 1815. Before the rise of Bonaparte, however, the French Army never comprised a dragoon unit having 'guard' status.

During the campaign of 1805, which culminated in Napoleon's victory at Austerlitz, the dragoon regiments of the Grande Armée performed particularly well and were one of the key factors behind the final triumph of the emperor. Consequently, Napoleon decided that the dragoons should also have the honour of being represented within his Imperial Guard. According to a decree of 15 April 1806, which created the Dragoons of the Imperial Guard, the new corps comprised four squadrons with two companies each. The regimental staff of the new unit was made up of the following elements: one colonel, two majors, three squadron-leaders, one paymaster, one captain-instructor, two adjutant-majors, five sub-adjutant-majors, four standard-bearers, three adjutant sub-lieutenants, five medical officers, one instructor, one quartermaster, two veterinary officers, four assistant-veterinaries, one trumpet-major, three trumpet-corporals, one kettle-drummer, two master-farriers and six master-craftsmen. The individual companies comprised one captain, one first lieutenant, two second lieutenants, one sergeant-major, eight sergeants, one quartermaster, ten corporals, three trumpeters, two farriers and ninety-six troopers. In addition to the four ordinary squadrons, there was also a fifth one of Velites, like in the Mounted Grenadiers and Mounted Chasseurs. In order to form the new dragoon unit of his Imperial Guard, Napoleon ordered each of the thirty regiments of dragoons of the French Army to send twelve of their best men (having at least ten years of service) to Paris. The officers and NCOs of the new corps were taken from the existing cavalry corps of the Imperial Guard.

The organization of the Regiment of Dragoons was partly slowed down by the outbreak of war between France and Prussia in 1806; after the end of the hostilities, however, Napoleon could complete the formation of his new unit. By 1807, the Dragoons of the Imperial Guard were fully operative and some of them were able to join the Grande Armée at the decisive Battle of Friedland. In September 1806, Napoleon had created another new cavalry unit inside the Imperial Guard, the short-lived Gendarmerie d'Ordonnance. This consisted of 400 soldiers, assembled into two squadrons with two companies each, all equipped as light cavalry. These came from the noble families of France and thus were rich gentlemen with great personal ambition. The emperor raised the Gendarmerie d'Ordonnance with the hope that the corps could attract the best elements of the aristocratic families, whose military contribution to the French cause had been very uneven since the creation of the Republic in 1792. As we have seen, the French Royal Guard had comprised a Gendarmerie made up of nobles until a few years before the outbreak of the Revolution. Napoleon now attempted a revival of this institution, but with little success. After taking part in the Polish campaign of 1807, the Gendarmerie d'Ordonnance was disbanded and its members were assigned to the other horse units of the Imperial Guard, including the Regiment of Dragoons. The latter, in contrast to the Gendarmes, soon became a solid military institution and a popular component of the Imperial Guard. This was in part the result of a peculiar episode that took place in Paris, during a military parade, in the closing months of 1807. The Empress Josephine, wife of Napoleon, was struck by the elegance of the Dragoons of the Imperial Guard and decided to become their patroness: as a result, from that moment, the regiment was commonly known as the Empress' Dragoons. During 1808 and 1809, the Regiment of Dragoons participated in several military actions in Spain and later took part in the Battle of Wagram against the Austrians. On all these occasions the Dragoons showed great combat capabilities and won the respect of the veteran soldiers from the Guard. Despite having been raised only during 1806–07, the Empress' Dragoons were part of the Old Guard like the Mounted Grenadiers and Mounted Chasseurs. Differently from the standard regiments of dragoons, that serving in the Imperial Guard was never used as an infantry corps and thus was a proper cavalry unit. After 1 July 1811, no further volunteers were admitted into the ranks of the Velites who were attached to the Regiment of Dragoons; those who were already part of the regiment were gradually absorbed into the Guard or line cavalry regiments after receiving commissions as officers. On 1 January 1812, all the remaining Velites who were still attached to the Regiment of Dragoons were grouped together to form a new 5th Squadron.

During the 1812 Russian campaign, the Empress' Dragoons were mostly kept in reserve along with the majority of the Imperial Guard's cavalry, and thus had few opportunities to show their valour. During the long retreat that followed the evacuation of Moscow, they suffered very heavy casualties like all the units of the Grande Armée and fought on several occasions against Cossacks who attacked the slow columns of the disintegrating army. In 1813, Napoleon had to reorganize his Regiment of Dragoons practically from scratch, mostly by using those veterans of the regiments of line cavalry who had survived. Such measures enabled him to reform the cavalry units of the Imperial Guard but deprived the line regiments of their most effective members. In January 1813, by using young conscripts, the emperor created a new 6th Squadron of Dragoons, whose members were known as Second Dragoons because they were not veterans and could not wear the *aiguillettes* like the soldiers of the other five squadrons. From an administrative point of view, only the officers and NCOs of the Second Dragoons were part of the Old Guard, while the troopers formed part of the Young Guard. These troopers, unlike their veteran comrades, received the same pay as the dragoons of the line regiments. The 1813 German campaign saw the participation of the Empress' Dragoons, who suffered heavy casualties in a series of minor engagements, as they did in the 1814 French campaign, when they fought even more heroically in order to defend their national soil.

When Louis XVIII became King of France after the first abdication of Napoleon, he decided to retain in service four cavalry regiments of the Old Guard but gave them new denominations: the Mounted Grenadiers became the Corps Royal des Cuirassiers de France, the Mounted Chasseurs were named the Corps Royal des Chasseurs a cheval de France, the Empress' Dragoons became the Corps Royal des Dragons de France and the Dutch Lancers were now the Corps Royal des Chevaulégers-lanciers de France. The Dragoons, now part of the Royal Guard, were organized like all the 'new' regiments on four squadrons with two companies each. When Napoleon returned to France, all the cavalry of the Royal Guard joined him and thus the four regiments listed above resumed their old names. The Dragoons continued to be organized on four squadrons, but Napoleon decided to re-form the Velites that had been disbanded several years before and attached 200 of them to the Regiment of Dragoons. The Dragoons fought at Waterloo and charged against the British infantry several times, like the rest of the Old Guard cavalry. After Napoleon's second abdication, the Empress' Dragoons were finally disbanded on 1 December 1815.

Soldier of the Empress' Dragoons.

Soldiers (left) and musicians (right) of the Empress' Dragoons.

Uniforms and equipment

From their foundation, the Dragoons of the Imperial Guard wore a very elegant dark green uniform whose most notable element was a copper helmet. The helmet was a mark of distinction for the unit: it was produced according to the contemporary Neo-Greek Minerve style, which was particularly popular in France, being adorned with a red plume and a black hanging mane. In addition, wrapped around the bottom part of the helmet was a band of leopard-skin that gave the dragoons' uniform an exotic appearance. The regiments of line dragoons had a copper helmet too, but this was simpler if compared with that used by the Empress' Dragoons (it did not have, for example, the band of leopard-skin). The basic uniform of the regiment was as follows: copper helmet; dark green tunic with dark green collar and round cuffs, white frontal lapels without piping, orange *contre-épaulettes* and orange *aiguillettes* on the right shoulder (these were not worn by the Second Dragoons); white waistcoat; buff trousers; black leather boots; and white belt equipment. The outfit was completed by a pair of white gloves, worn on most occasions by all members of the unit. The shabraque under the saddle was dark green with orange external edging, having an orange Imperial Crown in the back corner. Like the other cavalry corps of the Imperial Guard, the Empress' Dragoons had a simple campaign dress comprising a *surtout*, which was single-breasted and entirely dark green, including collar and round cuffs. The same orange *contre-épaulettes* and *aiguillettes* as on the tunic were worn with the *surtout*. On campaign, the *surtout* was frequently worn together with grey overalls (which were used instead of the usual buff trousers). During winter, a medium grey greatcoat with orange frontal frogging was worn over the uniform. The fatigue cap or *bonnet de police* of the dragoons was dark green, with orange piping and tassel, and also had an orange flaming grenade embroidered on the front. The trumpeters of the Regiment of Dragoons wore one of the most elegant uniforms of the entire French Army. This was light blue with white facings and consisted of the following elements: same helmet as the troopers but with light blue plume and white mane; light blue tunic with light blue collar and round cuffs piped in gold, white frontal lapels with external edges and buttonholes piped in gold, light blue-and-golden *contre-épaulettes*, plus light blue-and-golden *aiguillettes* worn on the right shoulder; white waistcoat; buff trousers; black leather boots; and white leather belt equipment. The shabraque was light blue with orange external edging, having an orange Imperial Crown in the back corner. In 1810, after Napoleon married Marie Louise of Habsburg, the uniform of the trumpeters was changed in honour of the new empress, who came from Austria, where most of the army was dressed in white and thus the trumpeters of the Empress' Dragoons also received a white uniform. This comprised the following: the same helmet as the troopers but with light blue plume and white mane; white tunic with light blue collar and round cuffs piped in gold, light blue frontal lapels with external edges and buttonholes piped in gold, light blue-and-golden *contre-épaulettes*, plus light blue-and-golden *aiguillettes* worn on the right shoulder; white waistcoat; buff trousers; black leather boots; and white leather belt equipment. The shabraque remained the same.

One of the Empress' Dragoons nicknames was the 'Men of bronze', because of their splendid helmets, although it should be noted that some soldiers in the regiment did not wear the helmet as headgear. These were the few sappers who were attached to the regimental staff of the unit. Like the line infantry and light infantry corps, all the dragoon regiments of the French Army included a small squad of sixteen sappers. These were combat engineers tasked with building field fortifications and destroying all the obstacles that could be encountered during the regiment's

Trumpeter of the Empress' Dragoons.

march. The dragoons could be employed, at least in theory, as infantrymen, and thus had a squad of sappers like the regiments of foot. The uniform of the sappers was as follows: black bearskin with orange cords and red plume; dark green tunic with dark green collar and round cuffs, white frontal lapels without piping, red *épaulettes*, orange *aiguillettes* and orange badge embroidered on the sleeves (consisting of two crossed axes under a flaming grenade); white waistcoat; buff trousers; black leather boots; and white belt equipment. Like all the sappers of the French Army, those of the Imperial Guard's Dragoons used various peculiar pieces of equipment: axe, white leather gloves and white leather apron. All sappers had long beards.

Chapter 7

The Polish Lancers

History and organization

The Regiment of Polish Lancers, the only foreign unit of the Old Guard's cavalry, was the most important corps of the Imperial Guard whose members were not French. As we have seen, Poland was wiped off the political map of Europe in 1807, with the territories of the former Polish-Lithuanian Commonwealth divided between three great military powers (Austria, Prussia and Russia). As a consequence, thousands of Polish exiles abandoned their country and went to France in order to continue the struggle against the invaders of their homeland. France had been at war with all the major European powers since 1792, and thus welcomed these courageous volunteers, most of whom were veterans with extensive military experience. The hundreds of Poles enlisting in the French Army were assembled into many independent 'Polish' units, which fought on several fronts from 1796. The Polish soldiers distinguished themselves from the outset with their incredible bravery and unquestionable loyalty towards France. They fought in every corner of Europe and were even sent to the French colony of Haiti, in the Americas, to crush a local rebellion of slaves. The Poles participated in the first Italian campaign of Napoleon (1796–97), during which they developed a special relationship with Bonaparte. Napoleon tried to recruit as many Polish soldiers as possible during his long military career, since he particularly appreciated the combat capabilities of these determined fighters. The Poles, in particular, were masters in the art of mounted skirmishing: for many centuries, their cavalrymen had been lightly equipped and armed with lances. Units of Polish lancers, known as uhlans, were included in all the major armies of Eastern Europe. These were respected for their great tactical flexibility, since they could operate as proper light cavalry but also conduct frontal charges with their lances. As a result, the Polish uhlans were a type of multi-tasking medium cavalry that were unrivalled in Europe.

In late 1806, Napoleon liberated most of Poland from the Russians, whom he later defeated at Eylau and Friedland. Consequently, he created a new independent state for his loyal Polish supporters (the Grand Duchy of Warsaw) in 1807, and could also recruit more Polish soldiers for his army. When the emperor entered Warsaw on 19 December 1806, the local community organized a guard of honour that was made up of young volunteers from the most important Polish noble families. Napoleon was so impressed by these fine soldiers that he decided to form a new unit inside his Imperial Guard, which was recruited in the territories of the newly liberated Poland. The new corps, according to the Emperor's intentions, was structured on just four companies with 120 men each. On 6 April 1807, the Regiment of Polish Light Horsemen was officially created, thanks to the decisive support of the new Polish government. The new unit was larger than the four companies originally required by the emperor, since it comprised four squadrons with two companies each. The regimental staff was made up of the following elements: one colonel, two colonel-majors, four squadron-leaders, one quartermaster-treasurer, one captain-instructor, two adjutant-majors, four sub-adjutants, one standard-bearer, four medical officers, one sergeant-major, one sergeant-wagonmaster, one veterinarian, two assistant-veterinarians, one trumpet-major, two trumpet-corporals, one master tailor, one master trousermaker, one master bootmaker, one master armourer, one master saddler, one master spurrier and two master farriers. A single company included one captain, two first-lieutenants, two second-lieutenants, one sergeant-major, six sergeants, one quartermaster, ten corporals, three trumpeters, two farriers and ninety-seven troopers. To become part of the Regiment of Polish Light Horsemen, a volunteer had to be a landowner or the son of a landowner. The cadres of the new corps comprised a number of French officers as well as several Polish veterans who had already served in the French Army. The Polish Light Horsemen completed their formation and joined the French Army in 1808, when Napoleon was mobilizing it for the invasion of Spain.

After signing the Treaty of Tilsit with Russia during the previous year, Napoleon decided to impose the so-called 'Continental System' on Europe. This consisted of closing all the ports of the continent to British merchant ships, in an attempt to destroy the economy of Great Britain. The Emperor of the French had all the resources to achieve this ambitious objective: his military forces had reached the peak of their power and seemed impossible to defeat, while most of the European states were under his direct control or were loyal allies of the French Empire. In Central Europe, in 1806, Napoleon had created the Confederation of the Rhine, a league of German states that were all allied with France and included the newly organized Kingdom of Westphalia, which was ruled by one of the emperor's brothers. In Italy, except for Sardinia and Sicily, Napoleon was dominant and controlled both the Kingdom of Italy (of which he was the supreme monarch) and the Kingdom of Naples (which was ruled by his brother Joseph). In the north, the Kingdom of Denmark-Norway was an ally of France, while in Eastern Europe, the newly established Grand Duchy of Warsaw supported the French with all its resources. To close the whole European continent to British ships, however, Napoleon had to assume control over another two countries: Spain and Portugal. Spain had been an ally of France for several years and was guided by a weak monarch, but while Portugal was a small country, it had extremely strong links – both political and commercial – with Great Britain. The Portuguese had no intention of becoming part of Napoleon's Continental System, and strove hard to resist French pressure. The only way for Bonaparte to crush the

Soldier of the Polish Lancers.

resistance of the Portuguese was to invade their country, and to do this French armies had to cross Spain. Napoleon negotiated with Spain to obtain permission for his troops to march across Spanish territory, after which a joint Franco-Spanish military force invaded Portugal in 1807, although Napoleon remained suspicious of his Spanish allies' real intentions. He posted garrisons in all the key locations of Spain and started to plan an invasion of the Iberian state. Some French troops were sent to Madrid, and the emperor later took the Spanish royal family into captivity at Bayonne in southern France. At this point, Napoleon forced Carlos IV, the Spanish monarch, to abdicate in favour of his son and thus practically assumed control of Spain's political life.

Such measures were too much for the Spanish population and caused great unrest throughout the peninsula: revolts broke out in several locations, most notably in Madrid, where the French garrison suffered heavy casualties after being attacked by thousands of civilian insurgents. Some days after these events, Napoleon decided to put his brother Joseph on the Spanish throne and military operations officially commenced between French troops and the Spanish Army. Things began badly for the French. On 22 July 1808, a French army of 18,000 soldiers was defeated by the Spanish at the Battle of Bailén and forced to capitulate, while in August, the British landed an expeditionary force in Portugal under the command of Wellesley – the future Duke of Wellington – and defeated the French troops that were stationed in the country. The French military situation in the Iberian Peninsula was deteriorating rapidly, forcing the emperor to act. He duly assembled a massive army and assumed command of military operations in Spain. After grouping his forces at Burgos, Napoleon moved on Madrid. To reach the Spanish capital, he was forced to cross the mountain ranges of Castile by marching across the mountain pass of Guadarrama or that of Somosierra. The latter was the shortest route to advance on Madrid, but it consisted of a narrow gorge that was well-defended by a Spanish army. The emperor had no idea of the effectiveness of the Spanish defences, and was surprised to learn that there were 20,000 enemy soldiers with sixteen guns guarding the mountain pass. Napoleon had no choice but to attack the entrenched Spanish troops with his infantry, whose advance was very slow and obtained very little during the early phase of the encounter. Since no outflanking manoeuvre could be attempted due to the nature of the terrain, it seemed that the French would be blocked at Somosierra for some time. However, on 30 November, Napoleon decided to launch a frontal cavalry charge against the Spanish artillery batteries that defended the mountain pass. The corps that was chosen to conduct this 'suicide' operation was the 3rd Squadron of the Polish Light Horsemen, which was attached to the French Army in Spain. For the Polish soldiers of the Imperial Guard, this was the first occasion to show their courage; they had no hesitation in charging the Spanish positions at full speed, and after a bloody but rapid combat, the 125 Poles were able to capture all sixteen entrenched artillery guns and open the way for a general advance of the French. Napoleon, shocked by the courage of his Polish guardsmen, took off his hat in front of them after the battle and said: 'You are worthy of my Old Guard! Honour to the bravest of the brave!'

After the end of the 1808 campaign, Napoleon decided to reorganize his Regiment of Polish Light Horsemen and re-equip it with lances, according to the traditional Polish military fashion of the uhlans. At that time the French Army had a single unit of lancers, another Polish regiment that was part of the so-called 'Vistula Legion'; this was a foreign corps, made up of several different Polish units. The emperor, however, had seen the great potential of the uhlans deployed by his enemies – Austria and Russia, in particular – and wanted to expand the lancer component of his army. The Regiment of Polish Light-Horsemen received the new denomination of Regiment of Polish Light Horsemen-Lancers, and was trained in the use of the cavalry lance by instructors from the Lancer Regiment of the Vistula Legion. The adoption of a new main weapon led to some minor changes in the uniform of the unit, since the decorative *aiguillettes* worn on the right shoulder had to be moved to the left side in order to facilitate the use of the lance. With their new equipment, the Polish Lancers fought with distinction at the Battle of Wagram in 1809, during which the Austrian uhlans caused severe losses to the French cavalry due to their mastery in the use of the cavalry lance. After this clash, Napoleon became even more convinced of the necessity of re-equipping part of his cavalry units with the latter weapon. Before 1810, the Regiment of Polish Lancers sent some detachments to serve in Spain, where French forces were experiencing increasing difficulties in crushing the local insurgents. These, known as *guerrilleros*, were masters in organizing ambushes and experts in mountain warfare; in addition, they could count on several efficient cavalry units equipped with lances that caused serious trouble to the French cavalry. To face the irregular lancers of the Spanish insurgents, Napoleon employed his Polish Lancers and even created a special corps of Mounted Gendarmerie, whose members were all armed with lances.

In March 1812, shortly before the start of the Russian campaign, the Regiment of Polish Lancers was expanded with the creation of a 5th Squadron. Like the other cavalry units of the Old Guard, it participated in the great invasion planned by Napoleon. By that time another unit of lancers, the Regiment of Dutch Lancers, had already been added to the cavalry of the Imperial Guard. After liberating Lithuania from the Russians, a third lancer corps of the Imperial Guard was recruited from local volunteers. Poland and Lithuania had formed a single 'Commonwealth' until 1795, and thus the Lithuanians also considered Napoleon as their liberator. The emperor tried to channel the great enthusiasm that followed his occupation of Lithuania in raising the third lancer unit for his Guard cavalry (the Lithuanian Lancers, which will be covered in one of the next chapters). During the first phase of the Russian campaign, the Polish Lancers had very few opportunities to show their valour; during the retreat from Moscow, however, they played a crucial role in operations by protecting (together with the Dutch Lancers) the flanks of the retreating French columns from attacks by marauding Russian Cossacks. The Cossacks were mostly armed with lances, so the Polish Lancers were among the few French cavalry units that could counter them effectively. At the end of the Russian campaign, due to the heavy casualties suffered, both the Polish Lancers and Lithuanian Lancers had very weak establishments. Since the Russians had invaded and occupied the Grand Duchy of Warsaw, thereby depriving him of the possibility to recruit more Polish soldiers, Napoleon had no choice but to disband the Lithuanian unit and use its members to fill the ranks of the Polish Lancers. After this organizational change, the unit started to be composed of six squadrons (three of which came from the Lithuanian Lancers) plus an attached squadron of Muslim Tatars who had been recruited in Lithuania (these will be covered in one of the following chapters). After the disbandment of the Grand Duchy of Warsaw's forces, several Polish veterans were absorbed into the French Army and some of these were used to create a 7th Squadron of the Regiment of Polish Lancers. During the German campaign of 1813, the Polish cavalrymen of the Imperial Guard fought with distinction on several occasions, but their unit was no longer composed of veterans as it had been in Russia. In December 1813, the number of squadrons in the Regiment of Polish Lancers was reduced to four, since three of them were used to form the new 3rd Regiment of Scouts of the Imperial Guard (see following chapters for more details).

With the first abdication of Napoleon in 1814, the Regiment of Polish Lancers was disbanded by the restored French monarchy because it was a military unit made up of foreigners. One hundred veterans of the corps, however, did not return to Poland, choosing instead to follow their emperor into exile. They were the only cavalry of the 'Elba Battalion', the small private army of Napoleon that numbered just 1,000 soldiers. The Polish cavalrymen who served the emperor during his first exile were organized into two companies, of which only one was effectively mounted. When Napoleon returned to France in 1815, the Imperial Guard was hastily reorganized but the Polish Lancers could not be re-formed as an independent unit since there were no more Polish soldiers in the French Army. As a result, the emperor assigned his 100 Polish veterans to the Regiment of Dutch Lancers, which assumed the new name of the Light Horse-Lancer Regiment. The Poles made up the 1st Squadron of

Trumpeter of the Polish Lancers.

this unit, and with this new organization they fought at Waterloo. After Napoleon's defeat and second abdication, they were finally disbanded on 1 October 1815. During their years of service in the Imperial Guard, the Polish Lancers wrote some remarkable pages of valour and courage: due to their brilliant combat performances, they are still remembered today as one of the most important units in the military history of Poland.

Uniforms and equipment

The Polish Lancers, since their foundation, wore an elegant uniform in perfect Polish style. This comprised a *czapska* (the national cap of the Polish light cavalry, with a square top) and a *kurtka* (the peculiar tunic of the uhlans, with frontal lapels forming a single plastron and with short turnbacks). During the Napoleonic period, the basic dress of the Polish Lancers remained the same: red *czapska* with white edging to the outer seams, white plume, white metal badge with a Polish Cross, white cords, brass frontal plate bearing a letter 'N' on the front, black leather peak and brass chinscale; dark blue *kurtka* with red collar and red pointed cuffs, red frontal plastron with white piping on the external edges, red short turnbacks, white *contre-épaulette* worn on the left shoulder and white *aiguillettes* on the right shoulder; dark blue trousers with red double side-stripe; black leather boots; and white belt equipment. When introduced, the cavalry lance used by the regiment had a guidon in the two national colours of Poland, red and white. The shabraque was dark blue with red external edging piped in white, and had a letter 'N' under an Imperial Crown embroidered in white on the front corner and an Imperial Eagle embroidered in white on the back corner. On campaign, the precious *czapska* was protected by a black oilskin cover and the *kurtka* was replaced by an entirely dark blue single-breasted short jacket. The usual trousers could be replaced by dark blue overalls with red single side-stripe and black leather internal reinforcement. Sometimes the *kurtka* could also be worn on campaign, but in this case the frontal plastron was worn in reverse (with the internal dark blue side visible). During winter, an entirely light grey greatcoat was used, while in barracks the *czapska* was replaced by a much more practical *bonnet de police* fatigue cap. This was red at the bottom and dark blue at the top, with white piping and frontal tassel. Until 1810, the trumpeters of the regiment were dressed as follows: red *czapska* with white edging to the outer seams, white plume, white metal badge with a Polish Cross, white cords, brass frontal plate bearing a letter 'N' on the front, black leather peak and brass chinscale; red *kurtka* with white collar and white pointed cuffs, white frontal plastron without piping on the external edges, white short turnbacks, white *contre-épaulette* worn on the right shoulder and white *aiguillettes* on the left shoulder (trumpeters did not have lances); red trousers with white double side-stripe; black leather boots; and white belt equipment. The shabraque was red with white external edging; it too had a letter 'N' under an Imperial Crown embroidered in white on the front corner and an Imperial Eagle embroidered in white on the back corner. In 1810, the following new dress was introduced for trumpeters: white *czapska* with red edging to the outer seams, white plume, white metal badge with a Polish Cross, silver-and-red cords, brass frontal plate bearing a letter 'N' on the front, black leather peak and brass chinscale; white *kurtka* with red collar and red pointed cuffs piped in silver, red frontal plastron piped in silver on the external edges and on the buttonholes, red short turnbacks, silver-and-red *contre-épaulette* worn on the right shoulder and silver-and-red *aiguillettes* on the left shoulder; red trousers with white double side-stripe; black leather boots; and white belt equipment. The shabraque was still red with white external edging, and had a letter 'N' under an Imperial Crown embroidered in white on the front corner and an Imperial Eagle embroidered in white on the back corner.

Chapter 8

The Dutch Lancers

History and organization

The Dutch Lancers only became part of the Imperial Guard in 1810, when the Kingdom of Holland ruled by Louis Bonaparte was officially annexed to the French Empire. During its short-lived existence (1806–10), the Kingdom of Holland had a sizeable army, which included a Royal Guard that was made up of several units. One of these, probably the best of the mounted corps, was a Regiment of Hussars, part of which, like several regiments of the Dutch Army, served with the French armies in Spain and made a very good impression on its allies. When the Dutch Royal Guard ceased to exist, Napoleon decided not to disband the Regiment of Hussars and instead transformed it into the 2nd Regiment of Lancers of his Imperial Guard. At the moment of their inclusion into the French Army, the Dutch Lancers were organized on four squadrons with two companies each. In total, the unit comprised the following elements: eleven staff officers, six captains, sixteen lieutenants, sixteen sub-lieutenants, 173 NCOs/trumpeters and 672 troopers. Each company had the following internal establishment: one captain, one lieutenant, two sub-lieutenants, one sergeant-major, one quartermaster, three trumpeters, two farriers, six sergeants, ten corporals and ninety-seven troopers. Sometime later, the number of squadrons was increased to five. Except for a few French superior officers, the whole regiment was made up of Dutch professional soldiers. The official transformation from hussars to lancers was decreed on 13 September 1810, when Napoleon was gradually expanding the lancer component of his cavalry, after having seen the Austrian uhlans in action at the Battle of Wagram during the previous year. The Dutch cavalry were trained in the use of the cavalry lance by their comrades of the Polish Lancers. On 10 February 1811, the old Dutch uniforms of the corps were substituted by new ones in Polish style; these were red with dark blue facings, the opposite of those worn by the Polish Lancers that were dark blue with red facings. After receiving their new dress, the Dutch cavalrymen of the Imperial Guard started to be known as the Red Lancers.

During the first phase of the Russian campaign, the Dutch Lancers had very few opportunities to show their valour, but during the retreat from Moscow, they played a crucial part by protecting (together with the Polish Lancers) the flanks of the retreating French columns from attacks by Russian Cossacks. The Cossacks were mostly armed with lances, and the Dutch Lancers were among the few French cavalry units that could meet them on equal terms. By the end of the 1812 campaign, the Regiment of Polish Lancers had been almost completely destroyed and had to be rebuilt by Napoleon. The emperor had no choice but to use new French recruits to reorganize the unit, and thus this rapidly lost its distinctive Dutch character. Of the original Dutch officers and NCOs, in fact, only fifty remained in service. Despite this, thanks to the massive amount of new recruits that were available, the emperor was able to expand the establishment of the Red Lancers from five to ten squadrons. By the beginning of the 1813 German campaign, at least on paper, the regiment had an impressive strength of 2,500 men. From an administrative point of view, the five senior squadrons were part of the Old Guard, while the five junior ones formed part of the Young Guard. The Dutch Lancers fought with distinction of several occasions in 1813 and 1814, especially at the Battle of Hanau. The latter encounter took place on 30–31 October 1813 and involved a clash between what remained of the French Army (decimated after the Battle of Leipzig) and the Bavarian Army. Bavaria had been one of Napoleon's most loyal allies until the German campaign of 1813, but decided to change side when France's final defeat appeared imminent. Against all odds, the French crushed the Bavarians at Hanau, thanks to a charge by

Soldier (left), officer (centre) and trumpeter (right) of the Dutch Lancers.

the Red Lancers. With the restoration of the monarchy in 1814, the Red Lancers were retained in service as part of the French Royal Guard, but their establishment was reduced to four squadrons with two companies each. The five junior squadrons of the Young Guard were all disbanded. With the return of Napoleon in 1815, the Red Lancers joined the emperor's cause and became part of his re-formed Imperial Guard. The Guard now comprised a single Regiment of Lancers, which consisted of the Red Lancers (four squadrons) plus a single squadron of Polish Lancers. The unit fought with distinction at Quatre-Bras and later at Waterloo, where it participated in the futile cavalry charges commanded by Marshal Ney. On 30 August 1815, the Red Lancers were finally disbanded.

Uniforms and equipment

Initially, the Dutch Lancers retained their old hussar uniforms, which were red with dark blue facings and had a distinctive French cut: black shako with black cockade, black plume, yellow cords and brass frontal plate with the initials of Louis Bonaparte under a Dutch Crown; red tunic with dark blue collar and pointed cuffs, red frontal lapels piped in dark blue, additional yellow lace on the collar and on the buttonholes of the frontal lapels, yellow *contre-éepaulette* on the left shoulder and yellow *aiguillettes* on the right shoulder; dark blue waistcoat with yellow piping and frontal frogging; dark blue trousers with yellow piping and decorative 'Hungarian' knots embroidered on the front; black leather short boots with yellow edging and frontal tassel; and buff leather belt equipment. The shabraque was red with yellow external edging. The new dress prescribed in February 1811 retained the same basic colours but had a distinctive Polish cut: red *czapska* with yellow edging to the outer seams, white plume, national cockade, yellow cords, brass frontal plate bearing a letter 'N' on the front, black leather peak and brass chinscale; red *kurtka*' with dark blue collar and dark blue pointed cuffs, dark blue frontal plastron without piping, dark blue short turnbacks, yellow *contre-épaulette* worn on the left shoulder and yellow *aiguillettes* on the right shoulder; red trousers with dark blue double side-stripe; black leather boots; and white belt equipment. The cavalry lance used by the regiment had a guidon in red and white. The shabraque was dark blue with yellow external edging, and had a letter 'N' under an Imperial Crown embroidered in yellow on the front corner and an Imperial Eagle embroidered in yellow on the back corner. On campaign, the precious *czapska* was protected by a black oilskin cover and the *kurtka* was replaced by a medium blue double-breasted short jacket with red collar. The usual trousers could be replaced by dark blue overalls with red single side-stripe and black leather internal reinforcement. Sometimes the *kurtka* could also be worn on campaign, but in this case the frontal plastron was worn in reverse (with the internal red side visible). During winter, an entirely medium blue greatcoat was used, while in barracks the *czapska* was replaced by a more functional *bonnet de police* fatigue cap, which was dark blue at the bottom and red at the top, having yellow piping and frontal tassel. The junior squadrons of the regiment, belonging to the Young Guard, were dressed with reversed colours: their *kurtka* was dark blue with red facings and their trousers were dark blue with red double side-stripe. The trumpeters of the Dutch Lancers were uniformed as follows: white *czapska* with red edging to the outer seams, white-and-red plume, national cockade, golden-and-red cords, brass frontal plate bearing a letter 'N' on the front, black leather peak and brass chinscale; white *kurtka* with red collar and red pointed cuffs piped in gold, red frontal plastron piped in gold on the external edges and on the buttonholes, red short turnbacks, golden-and-red *contre-épaulette* worn on the right shoulder and gold-and-red *aiguillettes* on the left shoulder; red trousers with gold double side-stripe; black leather boots; and gold-and-red belt equipment. The shabraque was red with golden external edging, and had a letter 'N' under an Imperial Crown embroidered in gold on the front corner and an Imperial Eagle embroidered in gold on the back corner. On campaign, the trumpeters wore a much simpler uniform: white *czapska* with red edging to the outer seams, white-and-red plume, national cockade, gold-and-red cords, brass frontal plate with a letter 'N' on the front, black leather peak and brass chinscale; medium blue *kurtka* with red collar and red pointed cuffs piped in gold, red frontal plastron piped in gold on the external edges, red short turnbacks, gold-and-red *contre-épaulette* worn on the right shoulder and gold-and-red *aiguillettes* on the left shoulder; medium blue trousers with red double side-stripe; black leather boots; and white belt equipment. The shabraque was dark blue with gold external edging, and it too had a letter 'N' under an Imperial Crown embroidered in gold on the front corner and an Imperial Eagle embroidered in gold on the back corner.

Chapter 9

The German Lancers and the Lithuanian Lancers

Following the 1805 campaign that culminated in the Battle of Austerlitz, France assumed control over the small German Duchy of Clèves, which was ceded to Napoleon by Prussia. In 1806, the emperor decided to unite the Duchy of Clèves with the nearby Duchy of Berg (already under French control) in order to create a new Grand Duchy of Clèves-Berg. This was ruled by Joachim Murat, one of Napoleon's best generals and his most courageous cavalry commander who had married one of the emperor's sisters. The new German state was part of the newly created Confederation of the Rhine, a group of German princedoms that was under the indirect political control of France and also comprised the Kingdom of Westphalia (whose monarch was Jérôme Bonaparte, brother of Napoleon). Soon after assuming control of Clèves-Berg, Murat started to reorganize the military forces of his new realm and formed a first cavalry unit, which acted as his personal mounted bodyguard. This changed its name several times before adopting the definitive official title of the Regiment of Light Horsemen. The soldiers of this new corps were all volunteers and came from the most prominent families of Clèves-Berg. While raising his Light Horsemen, Murat also tried to create another cavalry unit made up of Polish soldiers; eventually, this project failed and the few Polish horsemen who had been recruited were absorbed into the Regiment of Light Horsemen. This unit, after completing its organization, comprised three squadrons with two companies each, plus one elite squadron of Garde du Corps (Bodyguards). In 1808, Murat left his Grand Duchy for southern Italy, having been appointed King of Naples by Napoleon, and consequently, the Regiment of Light Horsemen was broken up. One squadron was absorbed into the French Imperial Guard, two squadrons were reorganized as a Clèves-Berg light cavalry unit (Mounted Chasseurs) and the Garde du Corps was absorbed into the Neapolitan Army. In early 1809, the squadron of German Lancers that had been attached to the Imperial Guard was disbanded; at the same time, the Mounted Chasseurs of Clèves-Berg were given lances and thus were transformed into a regiment of lancers. On 17 December 1809, the latter unit was absorbed into the Imperial Guard in order to replace the defunct squadron of German Lancers. The unit served with distinction in Spain during the following years, to the point that in March 1812 a second regiment of Berg Lancers was formed in preparation for

Soldier of the German Lancers with the second uniform worn by this unit.

The German Lancers and the Lithuanian Lancers 101

Soldier of the Lithuanian Lancers (left) and of the Dutch Lancers (right).

the invasion of Russia. This campaign proved a disaster for the German Lancers of the Imperial Guard, since only two companies out of two whole regiments returned from Moscow. These were assembled into a single squadron that continued to serve with the French Imperial Guard until being disbanded in 1813 after the fall of the Confederation of the Rhine.

The Lithuanian Lancers were raised in July 1812 in Lithuania. Napoleon had just liberated the country from Russian rule during his advance on Moscow, and thus many local volunteers (from the most prominent families of Lithuania) decided to join the French. The new regiment had five squadrons with two companies each, and had much in common with the Polish Lancers, from the uniform to the social background of its members. The unit became the 3rd Lancer Regiment of the Imperial Guard, after the Polish Lancers and the Dutch Lancers. During the retreat from Moscow, the Lithuanian Lancers suffered severe losses, and Napoleon had no choice but to use their surviving members to fill the gaps in the ranks of the Polish Lancers. As a result, after an existence of just a few months, the 3rd Lancer Regiment of the Imperial Guard was disbanded.

Uniforms and equipment

The Light Horsemen of Clèves-Berg were uniformed in Polish style as lancers from their foundation; until 1808 they wore a white uniform, which was substituted by a new dark green one when Murat left Germany for Naples. This was the first uniform of the unit: red *czapska* with white edging to the outer seams, white plume, national cockade, white cords, brass frontal plate bearing a letter 'N' on the front, black leather peak and brass chinscale; white *kurtka* with red collar and red pointed cuffs, red frontal plastron without piping, red short turnbacks, white *contre-épaulette* worn on the left shoulder and white *aiguillettes* worn on the right shoulder; red trousers with white double side-stripe; black leather boots; and white belt equipment. The shabraque was red with white external edging. Trumpeters wore the same dress but with reversed colours. The new uniform introduced in 1808 was as follows: red *czapska* with white edging to the outer seams, red plume, national cockade, white cords, brass frontal plate with a letter 'N' on the front, black leather peak and brass chinscale; dark green *kurtka* with pink collar and pink pointed cuffs, pink frontal plastron without piping, pink short turnbacks and dark green shoulder straps piped in pink; dark green trousers with pink double side-stripe; black leather boots; and white belt equipment. The shabraque was pink with black-and-white external edging. The new cavalry lance given to the regiment had a guidon in red and white. Trumpeters had the same uniform but with additional stripes of yellow livery on the sleeves and outer seams of the *kurtka*.

The Lithuanian Lancers were uniformed quite similarly to the Polish ones: red *czapska* with yellow edging to the outer seams, white plume, yellow cords, brass frontal plate with a letter 'N' on the front, black leather peak and brass chinscale; dark blue *kurtka* with red collar and red pointed cuffs, red frontal plastron with yellow piping on the external edges, red short turnbacks, yellow *contre-épaulette* worn on the left shoulder and yellow *aiguillettes* on the right shoulder; dark blue trousers with red double side-stripe; black leather boots; and white belt equipment. The cavalry lance used by the regiment had a guidon in the national colours of Poland-Lithuania, red and white. The shabraque was dark blue with red external edging piped in yellow; it had a letter 'N' under an Imperial Crown embroidered in yellow on the front corner and an Imperial Eagle embroidered in yellow on the back corner. The trumpeters of the regiment wore the following dress: white *czapska* with golden edging to the outer seams, white-and-red plume, golden cords, brass frontal plate with a letter 'N' on the front, black leather peak and brass chinscale; red *kurtka* with white collar and white pointed cuffs piped in gold, white frontal plastron with gold piping on the external edges, white short turnbacks, gold *contre-épaulette* on the right shoulder and gold *aiguillettes* on the left shoulder; dark blue trousers with gold double side-stripe; black leather boots; and white belt equipment. The shabraque was red with gold external edging, and had a letter 'N' under an Imperial Crown embroidered in gold on the front corner and an Imperial Eagle embroidered in gold on the back corner.

Chapter 10

The Guards of Honour and the Scouts

After the Russian campaign of 1812 Napoleon had to rebuild his armed forces from scratch as so many of his beloved veterans had died in the winter storms of Russia. The losses suffered by the Grande Armée during the retreat from Moscow had been immense, in terms of men and horses; as a result, the emperor was obliged to fight the 1813 German campaign with a very limited number of cavalry units. To ease this serious problem, Napoleon decided to create four new cavalry regiments that were recruited from young men of the richest French families. The emperor had already tried to do something similar in 1806 with the formation of the Gendarmerie d'Ordonnance, but this first experiment had failed. The aristocratic families of France had never supported the Napoleonic regime with great enthusiasm, but in 1813 the French Empire was on the verge of collapse and Napoleon had no choice but to use all the resources that were still available. Finding horses in order to form new cavalry units was extremely difficult, as was training new cavalry recruits effectively. The emperor had no time to do such things, so he badly needed new soldiers who could enter the ranks of the French Army with their own horses and who already knew how to ride properly. New volunteers with such characteristics, who could also pay for their own uniforms and equipment, could only be found in the aristocratic families of the French Empire. As a result, the four new cavalry regiments raised by Napoleon were made up of young gentlemen, and were subsequently named the Guards of Honour. These were officially created on 3 April 1813 with the enacting of an Imperial decree, according to which each of the new regiments comprised at least ten squadrons with two companies each, plus a sixty-five-strong regimental staff. In total, the four units were intended to provide 10,000 well-equipped and well-mounted soldiers to Napoleon, who would in due course provide the leadership cadres for the rebuilding French Army. The volunteers for the Guards of Honour were mostly aged 19–30, but a number of older men were also admitted into the new regiments. The unit was equipped as light cavalry and wore hussar-style uniforms. However, the response of the French nobility to Napoleon's call to arms was not very enthusiastic, and the new Guards of Honour therefore had to be recruited mostly from minor aristocratic families or from the upper-middle class of the French Empire: the sons of citizens who paid the highest income taxes in

The Guards of Honour and the Scouts

Soldier of the 1st Regiment of Honour Guards.

their home department or city, for example, were permitted to enlist in the regiments of Guards of Honour. To encourage volunteers, Napoleon introduced various incentives: the pay for members of the new corps was the same of the Old Guard's Mounted Chasseurs; in addition, after 12 months' service in the Guards of Honour, a recruit would receive a commission as sub-lieutenant in the French Army.

The four regiments were recruited not only from French citizens living in France, but also from those who resided in other parts of the French Empire. Each unit was recruited from a different geographical area: the 1st Regiment from the districts of Paris, Caen, Rouen, Lille, Brussels and Rome; the 2nd Regiment from Mézières, Metz, Nancy, Strasbourg, Amsterdam, Dijon, Wesel, Mainz and Genoa; the 3rd Regiment from Toulouse, Bordeaux, La Rochelle, Rennes, Périgueux, Tours, Florence and Groningen; and the 4th Regiment from Besançon, Grenoble, Toulon, Montpellier, Lyon, Bourges, Bastia, Turin and Hamburg. Senior officers of all the regiments came from the great nobility of France, while junior officers were required to have a yearly income of at least 5,000 francs in order to be appointed. By November 1813, a total of 9,700 volunteers had been raised for service in the Guards of Honour, and thus the general establishment planned by Napoleon was practically reached. Most of the men for the new regiments came from the departments of France proper, as potential volunteers living in Italy or Germany showed no great enthusiasm to serve under Napoleon. In such areas of the empire, several minor aristocrats paid high sums of money to find proxies who could enlist as their replacements, even though this practice was against the law. In July 1813, at the request of the gentlemen who made up the new units, one servant/groom for each two guardsmen was admitted into the ranks of the Guards of Honour's units.

The Guards of Honour were the military product of a wealthy middle class that had gradually developed across the 130 departments of the French Empire and had greatly improved its economic position thanks to the victories of Napoleon. Now this social class, which had helped make the administration of the Empire run smoothly for many years, was ready to support the emperor in his final campaigns and hoped to preserve all the privileges that it had gained thanks to Napoleon. The young members of the new regiments obviously lacked combat experience and did not have a clear idea of military discipline, but they learned how to fight during the German campaign of 1813 and by the beginning of the following year, were an effective military force. The four regiments of the Guards of Honour, at least formally, were not part of the Imperial Guard, but each of them was attached to a cavalry unit of the Old Guard: the 1st Regiment to the Mounted Chasseurs, the 2nd Regiment to the Empress' Dragoons, the 3rd Regiment to the Mounted Grenadiers and the 4th Regiment to the Dutch Lancers. The Guards of Honour fought with great distinction during the

French campaign of 1814, which saw their participation in several important military actions. By the time of Napoleon's first abdication, the four regiments had suffered so many casualties that all their members grouped together could barely muster a single squadron. All the units of Guards of Honour were officially disbanded in July 1814, although a good number of the surviving guardsmen were promoted to the rank of sub-lieutenant, as promised by Napoleon, and joined the re-formed Gardes du Corps of the Royal Household.

During the disastrous Russian campaign of 1812, the Grande Armée suffered greatly from attacks by Cossacks, lightly armed mounted skirmishers who were

Soldier of the 3rd Regiment of Honour Guards.

Soldiers of the 1st Regiment of Scouts; the figure on the left is from the senior squadrons and the figure on the right is from the junior ones.

equipped with spears and were used to fighting with hit-and-run tactics. In late 1813, in preparation for the new military campaign that was to be conducted in France, Napoleon knew very well that he had to reorganize his cavalry by creating new corps that could fight against the Russian Cossacks on almost equal terms. The

The Guards of Honour and the Scouts

emperor needed a number of cavalry equipped with lances, who could conduct scouting and skirmishing operations on all terrains. Consequently, in December 1813, Napoleon ordered the formation of three new cavalry regiments inside the Imperial Guard; these were defined as Éclaireurs, or Scouts, and were part of the Young Guard. Each of the three new units was attached to one of the Old Guard's cavalry corps: the 1st Regiment to the Mounted Grenadiers, the 2nd Regiment to the Empress' Dragoons and the 3rd Regiment to the Polish Lancers. As a result, the new corps were also known as Éclaireurs-Grenadiers, Éclaireurs-Dragons and Éclaireurs-Lanciers. Each of the three regiments had four squadrons with 250 men each. The 3rd Regiment of Scouts was mostly recruited from Polish soldiers – former members of the Polish Lancers – and was dressed quite similarly to that unit. The 1st Regiment of Scouts was recruited from veterans of the Old Guard (two squadrons) as well as from new recruits (two squadrons). The veterans were part of the Old Guard and had a hussar-style uniform, while the recruits were part of the Young Guard and wore a different dress. The 2nd Regiment of Scouts was mostly made up of *postillons* (former drivers/couriers).

Soldier of the 1st Regiment of Scouts, wearing the uniform used by the senior squadrons of this unit.

Soldier of the 1st Regiment of Scouts, wearing the uniform used by the junior squadrons of this unit.

The Scouts of the Imperial Guard were all mounted on the small but sturdy horses of southern France, coming from the region of Camargue. These were robust and could travel long distances in any climatic condition. Napoleon had developed the idea of creating Scout units mounted on these horses since 1806, but for various reasons this had not been possible. A single unit of this kind was recruited in present-

Soldier of the 2nd Regiment of Scouts.

day Belgium during 1806, known as the Chevau-légers d'Arenberg from the name of its commander, but two years later this was transformed into a regular regiment of line cavalry's Mounted Chasseurs.

In 1813, after the retreat from Moscow, a new regiment of lightly equipped mounted lancers was created within the military forces of the Grand Duchy of Warsaw. The 900 members of this Polish unit (known as Krakus) were the equivalent of the Russian Cossacks and were recruited from the peasants of rural Poland, who rode small ponies known as *konias* and were commanded by members of the rural nobility. During the German campaign of 1813, the Krakus Regiment fought with great distinction on several occasions, facing the Cossacks and causing them significant losses. After the fall of the Grand Duchy of Warsaw, the Krakus were absorbed into the French Army and continued to fight for Napoleon until the end of the 1814 campaign. In general terms, they acted as a model for the creation of the Imperial Guard's Regiments of Scouts. Assembled into an independent brigade, like the four regiments of the Guards of Honour, they fought extremely well during the French campaign but were too few to effectively counteract the Russian Cossacks. All such units were disbanded with the restoration of the monarchy.

Uniforms and equipment

The Guards of Honour had two different uniforms: a parade one in hussar-style and a service one that looked very similar to the second uniform used by the Mounted Chasseurs of the Old Guard. Generally speaking, the colours of the Guards of Honour's uniform (dark green and red) were clearly inspired by those of the latter much more famous regiment. The parade dress consisted of the following elements: red shako with a stripe of white lace on the top, white cords, white metal frontal plate bearing an Imperial Eagle, national cockade, black leather peak, white metal chinscale, pompom in regimental colour and dark green plume with the top part in regimental colour; dark green dolman with red collar and red pointed cuffs piped in white, white piping to the bottom edges and white frontal frogging with five vertical rows of buttons; dark green pelisse with white edging to the outer seams and black fur lining; red trousers with white side-stripe and white 'Hungarian' knots embroidered on the front; red-and-white sash wrapped around the waist; black leather boots; and white belt equipment. Regimental colours were red for the 1st Regiment, medium blue for the 2nd Regiment, yellow for the 3rd Regiment and white for the 4th Regiment. Like all the units dressed in hussar style, the Guards of Honour had a sabretache bag: this was black with a white metal badge on the front, representing an Imperial Eagle. The shabraque worn under the saddle was dark green with red external edging. The service uniform was much simpler. It could be worn with the shako or with a simple black bicorn, and comprised the following elements: dark green tunic with red collar and red pointed cuffs, dark green frontal lapels piped in red, white *aiguillettes* on the right shoulder and white *contre-épaulette* on the right shoulder; red waistcoat piped in white with white frontal frogging; dark green trousers with white 'Hungarian' knots embroidered on the front; black leather boots; and white belt equipment. The grooms/servants assigned to the regiments of Guards of Honour had their own peculiar dress, which was quite simple: black shako with white metal frontal plate representing an Imperial Eagle, national cockade, red pompom and small tuft in regimental colour; blue-grey tunic with dark green collar and pointed cuffs, blue-grey shoulder straps and frontal plastron piped in dark green;

blue-grey trousers with dark green 'Hungarian' knots embroidered on the front; black leather boots; and white belt equipment. The trumpeters were initially dressed like the other troopers of their regiments, except for having additional stripes of yellow livery on the sleeves of the dolman/pelisse and the colours of the shako's plume being inverted. Later, the trumpeters of the four regiments received the following uniform: black busby with pompom in regimental colour, dark green plume with the top part in regimental colour and red soft 'bag' with white piping and tassel; light blue dolman with red collar and pointed cuffs piped in white and white frontal frogging with five vertical rows of buttons; light blue pelisse with white frogging and white edging to the outer seams, plus black fur lining; red-and-white sash wrapped around the waist; red trousers with white piping and white 'Hungarian' knots embroidered on the front; black leather boots; and white belt equipment.

The Gendarmerie d'Ordonnance of 1806 was dressed quite similarly to the later Guards of Honour: black shako with national cockade, white plume, silver cords and white metal frontal plate showing an Imperial Eagle; dark green tunic with dark green collar and pointed cuffs, dark green frontal lapels without piping, silver *contre-épaulette* on the right shoulder and silver *aiguillettes* on the left shoulder; red waistcoat with silver frogging and piping; dark green trousers with white piping and white 'Hungarian' knots embroidered on the front; black leather boots; and black leather belt equipment piped in red. Trumpeters wore this same dress, but with black busby (having white plume and light blue soft 'bag') and with light blue facings to the tunic (collar, pointed cuffs and frontal lapels). The short-lived Gendarmerie d'Ordonnance also featured a single company on foot, whose uniform was exactly like that described above except for the headgear, which was a black bicorn with silver external edging and white plume. The drummers of this infantry company had light blue tunics instead of dark green ones.

Each of the three Scout Regiments of the Imperial Guard had a peculiar uniform, but all units were equipped with cavalry lances, which had a guidon in red and white. The 1st Regiment used two different kinds of dress: one for the senior squadrons of the Old Guard and one for the junior squadrons of the Young Guard. The senior squadrons' uniform was as follows: black shako with national cockade, white metal frontal plate representing an Imperial Eagle, red top band, white metal chinscale and dark green-and-red plume; dark green dolman with red collar and red pointed cuffs piped in white and white frontal frogging with five rows of vertical buttons; dark green pelisse with white frogging and white edging to the outer seams, plus black fur lining; red-and-white sash wrapped around the waist; dark green trousers with red piping; black leather boots; and white belt equipment. A black sabretache had a white metal Imperial Eagle on the front. The shabraque was dark green with white external

Soldier of the Mounted Gendarmes d'Ordonnance.

The Guards of Honour and the Scouts 115

Soldier of the Foot Gendarmes d'Ordonnance.

edging and a white Imperial Eagle embroidered on the back corner. The uniform of the junior squadrons was as follows: black shako with national cockade, white metal frontal plate representing an Imperial Eagle, red top band, white metal chinscale and dark green-and-red plume; dark green tunic with red piping to collar and pointed cuffs, dark green shoulder straps piped in red and dark green frontal lapels piped in red; grey trousers with double side-stripe and black leather internal reinforcements; black leather boots; and white belt equipment. A black sabretache had a white metal Imperial Eagle on the front. The shabraque was the same as for the senior squadrons. Trumpeters of all squadrons wore light blue pelisse, light blue dolman and light grey trousers. The 2nd Regiment was dressed as follows: crimson cylindrical shako with orange cords, national cockade, light blue pompom and white plume; dark green single-breasted jacket with crimson short turnbacks, crimson collar and pointed cuffs piped in dark green and dark green shoulder straps piped in crimson; dark green trousers with crimson double side-stripe and black leather internal reinforcements; black leather boots; and white metal belt equipment. The shabraque was dark green with crimson external edging. Trumpeters had the same uniform, but with a light blue jacket having gold piping to collar and pointed cuffs. The 3rd Regiment was uniformed exactly like the Polish Lancers, but had a white pompom on the *czapska* instead of the plume and wore a white-and-black sash wrapped around the waist. The standard dark blue trousers of the Polish Lancers were usually replaced by grey overalls, having black leather internal reinforcements. Trumpeters wore the same dress as their equivalents from the Polish Lancers, but with an orange pompom on the *czapska* instead of the plume and with a light blue *kurtka* having red facings piped in silver (collar, pointed cuffs and frontal plastron).

Chapter 11

The Mamelukes and the Tatars

After victory in the Battle of the Pyramids in 1798, the superior officers of the French army in Egypt recruited small numbers of local Mamelukes as their personal guides. These men, despite having been recently defeated by the French, served very well as scouts and on some occasions even saved the lives of officers to whom they were assigned by acting as bodyguards. Generals of division could have a maximum of ten Mameluke orderlies, while Generals of Brigade could have six. By February 1800, there were some 280 auxiliary Mamelukes serving with the French in Egypt. In July of the same year, the French organized the first independent auxiliary corps entirely made up of local soldiers, with two companies of Syrians and one of Mamelukes. Each of these three mounted companies comprised the following elements: one squadron leader, one captain, one lieutenant, two sergeants, four corporals and ninety-one troopers. On 26 October 1800, the three independent companies were combined in order to form a Regiment of Mamelukes. Mamelukes were already extremely popular in France because of their exotic clothes and incredible disdain for death in battle. Napoleon admired them and appreciated their combat capabilities – they were born light cavalrymen, whose tactical skills were unrivalled – as well as their incredible loyalty. When the French troops in Egypt were eventually defeated by the British, long after Napoleon had abandoned North Africa, all the Mamelukes who had collaborated with the invaders were permitted to leave for France together with their families. Of the original Regiment of Mamelukes, only two weak squadrons remained, which arrived in France on 29 September 1801.

Napoleon, who was by now First Consul of France, decided to raise a military unit from the refugees who had left the Levant. Initially, Napoleon wanted to create a squadron with 240 men, but was only able to recruit a single company. This was later expanded, thanks to the arrival of new recruits from the Levant, to become a squadron with two companies. The corps was admitted into the Consular Guard, and thus had an elite status from the beginning. All the NCOs and troopers of the unit were given 1,600 francs to dress and equip themselves, while officers received 1,800 francs. Each Mameluke carried the following traditional 'native' weapons: one carbine, one blunderbuss, two pairs of pistols, one sabre with curved blade, one dagger and one mace; a veritable arsenal. In addition, one of the two companies was also to be armed with lances, although apparently this measure was never put into

Mameluke of the Imperial Guard.

The Mamelukes and the Tatars

Mamelukes on parade in Paris, with one of their distinctive standards.

practice. Once established, the Squadron of Mamelukes had a staff that comprised the following: one colonel, one captain, one quartermaster, one surgeon-major, one lieutenant-instructor, one adjutant, one veterinary, one corporal-trumpeter, one master-saddler, one master-sailor and one master-bootmaker. Each of the two companies included one captain, one first lieutenant, one second lieutenant, one sub-lieutenant, one sergeant-major, four sergeants, one quartermaster-corporal, eight

Soldier of the Lithuanian Tatars, wearing the first uniform of this unit.

corporals, two trumpeters, one farrier and fifty-nine troopers. The Squadron of Mamelukes was attached to the Regiment of Mounted Chasseurs of the Consular Guard in January 1804, by which time its composition corresponded to that of a single company, since it was becoming increasingly difficult to find 'true' Mamelukes to serve in the corps.

In 1805, the Mamelukes fought with great distinction at the Battle of Austerlitz, counter-charging with the Mounted Grenadiers and Mounted Chasseurs against the cavalry of the Russian Imperial Guard. With their *tougs* standards at their head, the Mamelukes also took part in the great cavalry charge led by Murat at the Battle of Eylau. The Company of Mamelukes fought at Madrid against local insurgents in 1808, suffering significant losses; as a result, from 1809, French soldiers started to be admitted into the ranks of the Mamelukes in order to fill vacancies. The Company of Mamelukes took part in the 1812 invasion of Russia with the rest of the Imperial Guard, but by the end of the campaign, very little remained of the unit. Consequently, in the early months of 1813, Napoleon had to rebuild the unit almost from scratch. The emperor doubled the original establishment of the Mamelukes, as he did with the Regiment of Mounted Chasseurs, so the re-formed 'Egyptian' unit consisted of one squadron with two companies. The first company comprised a number of veterans who had returned from Russia and thus was part of the Old Guard;

Soldier of the Lithuanian Tatars, wearing the second uniform of this unit.

the second was made up of young French recruits and was part of the Young Guard. The Mamelukes continued to fight for Napoleon until the end of the 1814 campaign, when their corps was abolished. They were re-formed as a squadron in 1815 and fought at Waterloo before being disbanded.

In addition to the more famous Mamelukes, the Imperial Guard also included another cavalry unit made up of Muslim soldiers: the Tatars. These started to be raised in June 1812, when Napoleon liberated Lithuania from the Russians during his advance on Moscow. Since the Middle Ages, a warlike community of Muslim Tatars (descendants of the Mongols) had always fought in the military forces of the Polish-Lithuanian Commonwealth as crack light cavalrymen. Napoleon badly needed horsemen armed with lances who could fight against the Russian Cossacks on something like equal terms, so he was enthusiastic about recruiting Tatars. By October 1812 there were enough men to form a Squadron of Lithuanian Tatars, which was made part of the Imperial Guard. The unit comprised the following elements: one squadron leader, one major, four captains, seven lieutenants and 110 NCOs/soldiers. The new unit, attached to the Lithuanian Lancers, was almost completely destroyed during the long retreat of the Grande Armée from Russia. As a consequence, in March 1813, the surviving Tatars were first absorbed into the Lithuanian Lancers and later into the Polish Lancers, being used to form the new 3rd Regiment of Scouts.

Uniforms and equipment

Since the foundation of their corps, the Mamelukes were permitted to wear their national dress, so did not have a regular uniform. The headgear of their traditional costume could be a *cahuk* (soft cap) or a *tarbush* (rigid cap), around which a cotton turban was wrapped. The soft cap and turban could be of many different colours, although the rigid cap was always red. A brass badge, representing a crescent, was often applied on the front of the headgear. This 'unit badge' was later modified, becoming a five-pointed star that surmounted a crescent. A pompom with a tuft or plume frequently adorned the headgear of the Mamelukes. The other main elements of a Mameluke's outfit were the *mantanna* (a tunic with long sleeves), the sleeveless waistcoat worn over the tunic (produced in two different versions, known as the *fermelet* and *yalet*) and the very baggy trousers, or *sharual*. All these items of dress could be of many different colours, the most popular being yellow, orange and green. A coloured sash was worn around the waist, and personal equipment included a special holster for two flintlock pistols (the *kubur*). The Mamelukes' boots, made from coloured leather, were barely visible under the baggy trousers. All the 'original' Mamelukes rode without spurs. All belt equipment was made from coloured leather, and the horses' harness was in raditional oriental style. The standards of the Mamelukes were also oriental; these were known as *tougs* and consisted of a horse tail hanging from a shaft. Trumpeters were dressed like the other Mamelukes. In 1813, the Mamelukes were completely reorganized and an increasing number of French recruits were included in their ranks, so the traditional outfit described above became more standardized. The headgear became a black shako with a white turban wrapped around its bottom part, while the tunic became dark blue for all troopers, and the waistcoat and trousers became red for all troopers. All garments continued to be richly decorated with coloured embroidering. The sash that was worn wrapped around the waist was medium blue. The shabraque became standardized too, being dark blue with red external edging. The Mamelukes received a new second uniform in 1813, which was in western-style and was much more comfortable to wear than the oriental-style dress for the new French recruits of the unit. Very similar to the second uniform of the Mounted Chasseurs, but dark blue, this comprised: black bicorn with decorative stripes of red lace and national cockade; dark blue tunic with dark blue collar and dark blue pointed cuffs piped in red, dark blue frontal lapels piped in red, red *contre-épaulette* on both shoulders and red *aiguillettes* on the left shoulder; red double-breasted waistcoat; dark blue trousers with red piping and black leather internal reinforcements; black leather boots; and black leather belt equipment. The shabraque was dark blue with red external edging. From 1813, the trumpeters of the Mamelukes were dressed in the new second uniform described above, but their tunic was medium blue instead of dark blue and it had additional red-and-gold piping to the facings (collar, cuffs and frontal lapels).

The Tatars were given a very ornate uniform in 1812, which looked similar to the traditional dress of the Mamelukes. It consisted of the following elements: black cylindrical shako with brass unit badge on the front representing a crescent, yellow turban wrapped around the bottom part and dark green 'soft' bag on the top having red piping and tassel; dark green oriental-style tunic with long sleeves, crimson collar and pointed cuffs piped in yellow plus yellow piping on the front; crimson waistcoat worn over the tunic, having yellow piping to the outer seams; dark green baggy trousers with crimson double side-stripe; yellow sash wrapped around the waist; black leather boots; and white belt equipment. The pennon of the lance was red and green. The shabraque was dark green with crimson external edging, having a letter 'N' under an Imperial Crown embroidered in yellow on the front corner and an Imperial Eagle embroidered in yellow on the back corner. In 1813, a new and much simpler dress was introduced for the Tatars of the Imperial Guard: same headgear as the previous uniform; red oriental-style tunic with long sleeves, red collar and pointed cuffs; dark blue waistcoat worn over the tunic, with having red piping to the outer seams; medium blue baggy trousers with green double side-stripe; black leather boots; and black leather belt equipment. The pennon of the lance became white and green. The shabraque was dark blue with yellow external edging.

124 Napoleon's Imperial Guard

Lithuanian Tatar (mounted) and Mameluke (on foot).

Chapter 12

The Sailors and the Gendarmerie

The only naval infantry unit of the Imperial Guard was created for the planned French invasion of Great Britain. It consisted of a single battalion with 737 *marins*, commanded by a capitaine de vaisseau and a capitaine de frégate. The ranks used in the corps were the same as the contemporary French Navy, and the musicians of the battalion were trumpeters (not drummers, as would be expected for an infantry unit). The Battalion of Sailors were paid like the cavalry of the Imperial Guard and wore a distinctive uniform in light cavalry style; as a result, one of their most popular nicknames was the 'naval hussars'. They usually served in small detachments and provided the personal bodyguard for Napoleon when the emperor travelled on a ship. In essence, the Battalion of Sailors represented the French Navy inside the Imperial Guard. The establishment of the Sailors was increased to 818 men in 1804, and a drummer was added to each of the five 'crews' (i.e. companies) that made up the unit. In July 1808, the Sailors of the Imperial Guard fought at the Battle of Bailén, during which their unit was practically destroyed. They were re-formed as a single 'crew' with 148 men in 1809. During the campaigns of 1805–09, the Sailors fought as normal infantrymen but also performed specific functions such as manning river flotillas or building bridges of boats. On 16 September 1810, Napoleon reorganized the corps, giving it a battalion structure with a total of eight companies. By the beginning of the Russian campaign in 1812, however, only five of the planned eight companies had been effectively formed. Two of these five 'crews' served with distinction in Russia during 1812 and in Germany the following year, while a single company took part in the French campaign of 1814 before the Battalion of Sailors was officially disbanded. A few *marins* followed Napoleon into his first exile and were attached to the Elba Battalion. In 1815, the Sailors were re-formed on a single company with ninety-four men, which was later enlarged to 150. They were attached to the engineers of the French Army, but disbanded again on 15 August 1815.

The Gendarmerie d'Elite was the military police corps of the Imperial Guard, having been originally formed to serve with the Consular Guard. It performed a series of important non-combat functions, including the following: guarding the Imperial residencies, providing trusted couriers to the emperor, escorting Napoleon's personal carriage, ensuring the security of the emperor and of his entourage during travels, providing escorts to dignitaries who visited the territories of the French Empire and

Soldier of the Battalion of Sailors in parade dress.

acting as the 'provost corps' of the Imperial Guard. On campaign, the Gendarmes were attached to the Old Guard's cavalry and had to guard prisoners as well as the trophies – such as flags – taken from the enemy. During the Russian campaign of 1812, the Gendarmes played a crucial role, gathering any laggards back into the retreating army. In 1805, the corps consisted of two mounted squadrons with two companies each, and one foot half-battalion with two companies, with a total of 630 men. They were all NCOs who came from the ordinary units of the National Gendarmerie. On 15 April 1806 the half-battalion on foot was disbanded. After the Russian campaign, the Gendarmerie d'Elite was expanded with the creation of another two mounted squadrons, which were made up of new recruits and thus were part of the Young Guard. With this expansion, the Gendarmes numbered 1,174 men. The two new squadrons were collectively known as 'Gendarmes-bis', or 'Second Gendarmes'. On 16 January 1814, a total of 160 cadets – known as 'Gendarmes-cadets' – were added to the Gendarmerie of the Imperial Guard. These were young aspirants with little military experience, like the former Velites who were attached to the Old Guard's units. With the restoration of the French monarchy, the Gendarmes were disbanded, but several of their senior members were absorbed into a new unit of the Royal Household (the Gendarmes des Chasses du Roi). With the return of Napoleon to France, the Gendarmes were reorganized, initially consisting of just one company with 100 men, which was later expanded to two companies with 250 men. On 26 September 1815, the Gendarmerie d'Elite was disbanded for a final time.

Soldier of the Battalion of Sailors in parade dress.

NCO of the Mounted Gendarmes on sentry duty.

Soldier (left), officer (centre) and drummer (right) of the Foot Gendarmerie.

Uniforms and equipment

The parade uniform of the Sailors of the Imperial Guard was as follows: black shako with brass frontal plate representing an Imperial Eagle, orange cords and top band, red pompom and plume; dark blue dolman with dark blue collar and red pointed cuffs piped in orange, golden *contre-épaulettes*, orange piping to the front of the dolman and orange frontal frogging with five vertical rows of buttons; dark blue trousers with orange piping and decorative 'Hungarian' knots embroidered on the front; black shoes; and black leather belt equipment. The musicians of the unit wore the same uniform as above, but in light blue instead of dark blue and with gold decorations instead of orange. On campaign, instead of the dolman, the Sailors could wear a simpler double-breasted jacket without frontal frogging, which had

Quartermaster of the Battalion of Sailors.

a dark blue collar and pointed cuffs piped in orange. The campaign jacket was used with a simplified version of the shako (without frontal plate and with just an orange pompom instead of the plume) and with entirely dark blue trousers. Officers were dressed quite differently from their men: black bicorn with national cockade, red plume and decorative stripes of golden lace; dark blue tunic with dark blue collar and dark blue pointed cuffs, gold lace on the collar and gold piping on the cuffs, dark blue frontal lapels without piping, golden *contre-épaulette* with *aiguillettes* on the right shoulder and golden epaulette on the left shoulder; red waistcoat with gold frontal piping and frogging; dark blue trousers with gold piping and gold 'Hungarian' knots embroidered on the front; black leather boots with gold edging and decorative tassel; and black leather belt equipment.

Until 1806, the Foot Gendarmes were uniformed as follows: black bicorn with national cockade, white edging and red plume; dark blue tunic with dark blue collar and red round cuffs, dark blue cuff flaps, red frontal lapels and red epaulettes; buff waistcoat and trousers; black leggings and shoes; and buff leather belt equipment. On campaign, the plume of the bicorn was removed and the tunic was replaced by a dark blue single-breasted *surtout* with red frontal piping. This was worn together with dark blue trousers. During winter months, an entirely dark blue greatcoat with white frontal frogging was used. In 1806, the Foot Gendarmes received a black bearskin as new headgear, which had white cords and red plume, being quite similar to that of the Foot Grenadiers. The drummers of the Foot Gendarmes were dressed like the other soldiers of their unit, but with uniforms in reversed colours (red with dark blue facings). Until 1806, the Mounted Gendarmes were uniformed as follows: black bicorn with national cockade, white edging and red plume; dark blue tunic with dark blue collar and red round cuffs, red frontal lapels, white *contre-épaulettes* and white *aiguillettes* on the left shoulder; buff waistcoat and trousers; black leather boots; and buff leather gloves and belt equipment. The shabraque was dark blue with white external edging and a white flaming grenade embroidered on the back corner. The Mounted Gendarmes received a black bearskin as new headgear in 1806: this had white cords and red plume, similar to that of the Mounted Grenadiers. On campaign, the tunic was replaced by a dark blue single-breasted *surtout* with red frontal piping, which was worn together with dark grey overalls. During the winter, an entirely dark blue greatcoat with white frontal frogging was worn. The trumpeters of the Mounted Gendarmes were dressed like the other soldiers of their unit, but with uniforms in reversed colours (red with dark blue facings). The collar, cuffs and frontal lapels of their tunics were piped in silver on the external edges and on the buttonholes, while the *contre-épaulettes* and *aiguillettes* of trumpeters were silver. All members of the Gendarmerie d'Elite had a dark blue *bonnet de police*, with white piping and frontal tassel, which was worn in barracks.

Soldier of the Mounted Gendarmes with parade dress.

Soldier of the Mounted Gendarmes with campaign dress (including *surtout*).

Chapter 13

The Artillery and the Train

According to the new organization introduced on 8 March 1802, the artillery of the Consular Guard consisted of just two mounted companies with four officers and eighty-five soldiers each. It was expanded in November 1803 and restructured on three divisions, each of which had the following pieces: two 6-pdrs, two 12-pdrs and two 6in howitzers. On 15 April 1806, the artillery of the new Imperial Guard was reorganized as a Regiment of Mounted Artillery with three squadrons of two companies each. A single company comprised ninety-seven gunners with four 4-pdrs and two 6in howitzers. On 12 April 1808, Napoleon created a new Regiment of Foot Artillery to boost the Imperial Guard's artillery component. The new unit was structured on six artillery companies plus one company of *pontoniers*, who were charged with constructing bridges. With the formation of the Regiment of Foot Artillery, the Mounted Artillery of the Imperial Guard was reduced to just two squadrons with two companies each. The single companies of foot artillery were equipped with six field pieces of 6-pdrs or 12-pdrs, plus two howitzers. Both the Foot Artillery and the Mounted Artillery were part of the Old Guard. On 9 June 1809, three new companies were added to the Regiment of Foot Artillery; these were made up of new recruits and thus belonged to the Young Guard. Officers and NCOs of these new companies came from the existing senior companies and thus were part (at least formally) of the Old Guard. Another junior company of foot artillery was formed on 12 December 1811, followed by another two on 2 January 1813. During 1813, the Regiment of Foot Artillery was greatly expanded with the creation of another ten junior companies, which were all made up of new recruits. The Regiment of Mounted Artillery was also expanded, with the addition of a third squadron and a single company made up of new recruits (which was part of the Young Guard). At the beginning of the Russian campaign, the artillery of the Imperial Guard had a total of ninety-six guns, with seventy-two manned by the foot gunners and twenty-four by the mounted gunners. With the restoration of the French monarchy, the artillery of the Imperial Guard was disbanded, but when Napoleon returned, it was reorganized on four companies of Mounted Artillery and six companies of Foot Artillery, plus one company of artillery artisans. On 28 May 1815, a new foot company of the Young Guard was organized, but it did not join the French Army in time and thus could not fight at Waterloo.

Soldiers of the Mounted Artillery Regiment, with second uniform (left) and with parade dress (right).

Soldiers of the Mounted Artillery (left) and of the Artillery Train (right).

The Imperial Guard also included various small technical corps that supported the artillery: the Artillery Train, the Wagon Train and the Engineers. An Artillery Train company, tasked with transporting the ammunition and equipment of the artillery, was organized in the Consular Guard on 8 September 1800. This was expanded to two companies in June 1802 and to four companies in November 1803, before being transformed into a battalion with six companies in April 1806. In 1807, a 2nd Battalion of the Artillery Train was organized, but this was soon absorbed into the line units of the French Army as a standard artillery train battalion. In October 1809, three companies were added to the remaining battalion, which was completely reorganized after the Russian campaign. It was restructured as a regiment in 1813 with three battalions, each of which had four companies. Sometime later, a fourth battalion was added to the regiment. In April 1813, this new battalion was detached to form a 2nd Regiment of the Artillery Train, which had three battalions like the 1st Regiment. Disbanded in 1814, the Artillery Train of the Imperial Guard was reorganized on nine companies (one of which was part of the Young Guard) for the Belgian campaign of 1815. The Wagon Train, tasked with transporting the materials and equipment of the Imperial Guard, was created on 15 April 1806 as a single battalion with six companies. It was enlarged with the addition of three new companies in March 1813, and was disbanded in 1814. The Wagon Train was re-formed in 1815 as a single squadron with 200 men. The Engineers of the Imperial Guard were formed in July 1811 in order to act as firemen for the Imperial residencies, consisting of a single company with six horse-drawn pumps. In 1812, four junior companies, which were part of the Young Guard, were added to the corps. During 1814, the Engineers of the Imperial Guard became a battalion with the addition of two new companies. Disbanded in 1814, they were reorganized in 1815 as a single company with 125 men.

Uniforms and equipment

The Mounted Artillery of the Consular Guard was dressed as follows: black bearskin with red plume, dark blue tunic with dark blue collar piped in red and red pointed cuffs, dark blue frontal lapels piped in red, red *contre-épaulettes* and red *aiguillettes* on the left shoulder; red double-breasted waistcoat; dark blue overalls with red piping and black leather internal reinforcement; and white leather belt equipment. The shabraque was dark blue with red external edging, and with a red flaming grenade embroidered on the back corner. Trumpeters wore the same uniform but in light blue rather than dark blue, and their headgear was a black busby with light blue-and-white plume. This uniform was replaced by a new one (in hussar-style) after the creation of the Imperial Guard, and now comprised: black busby with red plume, red cords and red 'soft' bag with red decorative tassel; dark blue dolman with dark blue collar piped in red and red pointed cuffs, plus red frontal frogging with three vertical rows of buttons; dark blue pelisse with red frontal frogging and red edging to the outer seams, and black fur lining; red-and-yellow sash wrapped around the waist; dark blue trousers with red piping and decorative 'Hungarian' knots embroidered on the front; black leather boots with red edging and frontal tassel; and white leather belt equipment. The shabraque was dark blue with red external edging and a red flaming grenade embroidered on the back corner. Like the Mounted Chasseurs, the Mounted Artillerymen had a second uniform: black busby with red plume, red cords and red 'soft' bag with red decorative tassel; dark blue tunic with dark blue collar piped in red and red pointed cuffs, dark blue frontal lapels piped in red, red *contre-épaulettes* and red *aiguillettes* on the left shoulder; dark blue waistcoat with red frontal piping and frogging; dark blue trousers with red piping and decorative 'Hungarian' knots embroidered on the front; black leather boots with red edging and frontal tassel; and white leather belt equipment. The parade dress of trumpeters comprised a white busby with light blue-and-white plume, red dolman, light blue pelisse (line with white fur) and light blue trousers. The second uniform of trumpeters included a black busby with light blue-and-white plume, light blue tunic with dark blue facings (collar, cuffs and frontal lapels all piped in gold), light blue waistcoat and trousers.

The Foot Artillery of the Imperial Guard wore the following uniform: black shako with brass frontal plate representing an Imperial Eagle, red cords, red top band, national cockade, red pompom and red plume; dark blue tunic with dark blue collar piped in red and red round cuffs, red cuff flaps, red epaulettes and dark blue frontal lapels piped in red; dark blue waistcoat and trousers; black leggings; and white leather belt equipment. In 1810, the shako was replaced by a black bearskin with red plume and cords, which was very similar to that worn by the Foot Grenadiers. The new companies that were formed as part of the Young Guard did not have the privilege of wearing the bearskin and thus used the standard shako described above. Drummers had gold piping to the facings of their uniform (collar, cuffs and frontal lapels); in addition, their collar and frontal lapels were red and not dark blue. All artillerymen wore a dark blue *bonnet de police* with red piping and red flaming grenade embroidered on the front when serving in their barracks. The Artillery Train's first uniform was quite simple: black bicorn with national cockade and red plume; iron grey tunic with dark blue collar and pointed cuffs piped in red, dark blue frontal lapels piped in red and red *contre-épaulettes*; white waistcoat and trousers; black leather boots; and white leather belt equipment. A new uniform was introduced in 1810: black shako with brass frontal plate representing an Imperial Eagle, national cockade, red top band, red plume and red cords; iron grey tunic with dark blue collar and pointed cuffs piped in red, dark blue frontal lapels piped in red and red *contre-épaulettes*, iron grey

The Artillery and the Train 139

Officer of the Foot Artillery Regiment.

Soldiers of the Foot Artillery Regiment.

waistcoat with red frontal piping and frogging; iron grey trousers with red piping and decorative 'Hungarian' knots embroidered on the front; black leather boots with red edging and frontal tassel; and white leather belt equipment. In 1813, a new tunic was introduced with the frontal lapels united to form a single plastron and the waistcoat was abolished. Until 1812, trumpeters were dressed like the other soldiers of their unit, but with a red shako having a white plume and with a medium blue uniform having dark blue facings; in 1812, they received the same hussar-style uniform as the Mounted Artillery's trumpeters.

The Wagon Train had a very simple uniform, which was similar to that of the Artillery Train: black shako with national cockade, white metal frontal plate

Soldier of the Artillery Train (left) and of the Foot Artillery (right).

representing an Imperial Eagle, white cords and red pompom; iron grey tunic with brown collar and round cuffs, iron grey cuff flaps, iron grey shoulder straps piped in brown and brown frontal lapels; iron grey waistcoat; white trousers; black leather boots; and white leather belt equipment. In 1813, a new tunic was introduced with the frontal lapels united to form a single plastron and the waistcoat was abolished.

Engineers of the Imperial Guard, comprising a drum-major (with red crest on the helmet) and two soldiers with the protective helmet/cuirass used during excavations.

Trumpeters had additional red-and-white piping to the facings of their tunic (collar, cuffs and frontal lapels). The Engineers of the Imperial Guard wore a simple but extremely elegant uniform: white metal helmet (that was later copied by most of the world's firemen corps) with a brass Imperial Eagle applied on the front, black crest, red plume and brass chinscale; dark blue tunic with black collar and round cuffs piped in red, black cuff flaps and frontal lapels piped in red, plus red epaulettes; dark blue waistcoat and trousers; black leggings; black shoes; and white leather belt equipment. Drummers had a red crest on the helmet instead of the black one and had gold piping to the facings of their tunic (collar, cuffs and frontal lapels).

The Artillery and the Train 143

Soldier of the Engineers.

Bibliography

Bucquoy, E.L., *Dragons et Guides d'Etat-Major* (Editions Grancher, 1980).
Bukhari, E., *Napoleon's Guard Cavalry* (Osprey Publishing, 1978).
Crowdy, T., *French Revolutionary Infantry 1789–1802* (Osprey Publishing, 2004).
Funcken, F. and Funcken, L., *Les Soldats de la Revolution Française* (Casterman, 1988).
Grant, C., *Foot Grenadiers of the Imperial Guard* (Osprey Publishing, 1971).
Haythornthwaite, P., *Imperial Guardsman 1799–1815* (Osprey Publishing, 1997).
Haythornthwaite, P., *Napoleon's Guard Infantry I* (Osprey Publishing, 1984).
Haythornthwaite, P., *Napoleon's Guard Infantry II* (Osprey Publishing, 1985).
Haythornthwaite, P., *Napoleon's Specialist Troops* (Osprey Publishing, 1988).
Jouineau, A. and Mongin, J.M., *The French Imperial Guard: Cavalry 1804–1815 (part 1)* (Histoire & Collections, 2003).
Jouineau, A. and Mongin, J.M., *The French Imperial Guard: Cavalry 1804–1815 (part 2)* (Histoire & Collections, 2005).
Jouineau, A. and Mongin, J.M., *The French Imperial Guard: Cavalry 1804–1815 (part 3)* (Histoire & Collections, 2007).
Jouineau, A. and Mongin, J.M., *The French Imperial Guard: The Artillery Train, the Wagon Train, the Administration, the Medical Service, the Headquarters Staff* (Histoire & Collections, 2007).
Jouineau, A. and Mongin, J.M., *The French Imperial Guard: The Foot Soldiers, 1804–1815* (Histoire & Collections, 2002).
Novarese, V.N., *La Guardia Imperiale Napoleonica: I Reggimenti della Vecchia e Media Guardia 1806–1813* (Ermanno Albertelli Editore, 1996).
Pawly, R., *Mounted Grenadiers of the Imperial Guard* (Osprey Publishing, 2009).
Pawly, R., *Napoleon's Dragoons of the Imperial Guard* (Osprey Publishing, 2012).
Pawly, R., *Napoleon's Guards of Honour 1813–1814* (Osprey Publishing, 2002).
Pawly, R., *Napoleon's Mamelukes* (Osprey Publishing, 2006).
Pawly, R., *Napoleon's Mounted Chasseurs of the Imperial Guard* (Osprey Publishing, 2008).
Pawly, R., *Napoleon's Polish Lancers of the Imperial Guard* (Osprey Publishing, 2007).
Pawly, R., *Napoleon's Red Lancers* (Osprey Publishing, 2003).
Pawly, R., *Napoleon's Scouts of the Imperial Guard* (Osprey Publishing, 2006).
Wilkinson-Latham, R., *Napoleon's Artillery* (Osprey Publishing, 1975).
Young, P., *Chasseurs of the Guard* (Osprey Publishing, 1971).

Index

Amiens, 9
Amsterdam, 106
Austerlitz, 19–20, 59, 68, 79, 99, 121

Bastia, 106
Batavian Republic, 22
Berg, 99, 102
Besançon, 106
Bordeaux, 106
Borodino, 24, 70
Bourges, 106
Brussels, 106

Caen, 106
Camargue, 110
Cent-Gardes Suisses, 1–2
Compagnie des Chevaux-Légers, 1–2
Compagnie des Gendarmes, 1–2

Dijon, 106

Eylau, 20, 59, 70, 86, 121

Florence, 40, 51, 106
Friedland, 20, 48, 79, 86

Gardes de la Manche, 1–2
Gardes de la Porte, 1–2
Gardes de la Prevote, 1–3, 30
Gardes du Corps, 1–2
Gardes Françaises, 1–3
Gardes Suisses, 2–3
Gendarmerie de France, 2
Genoa, 106
Grenadiers à Cheval, 1–2
Grenoble, 106
Groningen, 106

Hamburg, 106

Jena, 20

La Rochelle, 106
Leipzig, 48, 71, 96
Lille, 106

Louis Bonaparte, 22, 24, 41, 95, 97
Louis XIV, 1, 56, 77
Louis XVIII, 61–2, 72, 81
Lyon, 106

Madrid, 89, 121
Mainz, 106
Maison du Roi, 1, 7
Marengo, 7, 17, 57, 68
Metz, 106
Mézières, 106
Montpellier, 106
Moscow, 26, 61, 80, 91, 95, 102, 104, 111, 122
Mousquetaires du Roi, 1–2
Murat, 16, 59, 70, 99, 102, 121

Nancy, 106
Naples, 87, 99, 102
Nelson, 10
Ney, 72, 97

Périgueux, 106

Rennes, 106
Rome, 106
Rouen, 106
Roustam Raza, 8

Somosierra, 89
Strasbourg, 106

Toulon, 106
Toulouse, 106
Tours, 106
Trafalgar, 10
Tuileries, 3
Turin, 40, 51, 106

Versailles, 2

Wagram, 61, 70, 80, 90, 95
Waterloo, 29–30, 50, 62, 65, 72, 81, 93, 97, 122, 134
Wesel, 106
Westphalia, 87, 99